PRINCETON STUDIES IN INTERNATIONAL FINANCE

No. 62, August 1988

DEVALUATION, EXTERNAL BALANCE, AND MACROECONOMIC PERFORMANCE: A LOOK AT THE NUMBERS

STEVEN B. KAMIN

INTERNATIONAL FINANCE SECTION

DEPARTMENT OF ECONOMICS
PRINCETON UNIVERSITY
PRINCETON, NEW JERSEY

PRINCETON STUDIES
IN INTERNATIONAL FINANCE

PRINCETON STUDIES IN INTERNATIONAL FINANCE are published by the International Finance Section of the Department of Economics of Princeton University. While the Section sponsors the Studies, the authors are free to develop their topics as they wish. The Section welcomes the submission of manuscripts for publication in this and its other series. See the Notice to Contributors at the back of this Study.

The author of this Study, Steven B. Kamin, is an economist in the International Finance Division of the Federal Reserve Board in Washington. The views expressed here are the author's own and do not necessarily reflect the views of the Board of Governors or other members of its staff.

DWIGHT M. JAFFEE, *Acting Director*
International Finance Section

PRINCETON STUDIES IN INTERNATIONAL FINANCE

No. 62, August 1988

DEVALUATION, EXTERNAL BALANCE, AND MACROECONOMIC PERFORMANCE: A LOOK AT THE NUMBERS

STEVEN B. KAMIN

INTERNATIONAL FINANCE SECTION

DEPARTMENT OF ECONOMICS
PRINCETON UNIVERSITY
PRINCETON, NEW JERSEY

INTERNATIONAL FINANCE SECTION
EDITORIAL STAFF

Peter B. Kenen, *Director*
Ellen Seiler, *Editor*
Paul Knight, *Subscriptions and Orders*

Library of Congress Cataloging-in-Publication Data

Kamin, Steven, 1957-
    Devaluation, external balance, and macroeconomic performance : a look at the numbers / Steven B. Kamin.
    p.   cm.— (Princeton studies in international finance, ISSN 0081-8070 ; no. 62)
    Bibliography: p.
    ISBN 0-88165-234-2
    1. Devaluation of currency—Developing countries. 2. Balance of payments—Developing countries. 3. Developing countries—Economic conditions.
I. Title.   II. Series.
    HG1496.K36 1988
    332.4′14—dc19   88-22384
                                                                    CIP

Printed in the United States of America by Princeton University Press at Princeton, New Jersey.

International Standard Serial Number: 0081-8070
International Standard Book Number: 0-88165-234-2
Library of Congress Catalog Card Number: 88-22384

CONTENTS

LIST OF TABLES

LIST OF FIGURES

1 INTRODUCTION

The relative merits of currency devaluation in developing countries have been the subject of considerable debate in recent years. Analysts at international institutions, and particularly at the International Monetary Fund, have generally maintained that devaluation plays a positive and important role in balance-of-payments stabilization, while academic research has focused mainly on newly discovered contractionary and otherwise perverse effects of exchange-rate adjustment. Yet this debate over the efficacy of currency devaluation has been largely theoretical, bolstered at times by simulation analyses or case studies of particular devaluations. In 1971, by contrast, Richard Cooper surveyed twenty-four devaluations of the preceding two decades, assessing statistically the extent of the response of the balances of trade and payments, inflation, and the elements of aggregate demand. Surprisingly, there has been little effort in recent years to deepen and update his research, and the gap between our theoretical understanding and our empirical grasp of the devaluation process has never been wider.

This study fills part of that gap. Ideally, both theoretical and empirical analyses should be directed toward answering the fundamental question: What is the impact of devaluations on external balance and macroeconomic performance in developing countries? A proper answer requires, first, the compilation of "stylized facts" about the devaluation process and, second, the formulation of a consistent theoretical model showing the response of an economy to exchange-rate change. The theoretical model is clearly central to the explanation of how devaluations work, as well as to the estimation of the magnitudes involved. But the stylized facts, that is, the characterization of how economies, on average, have behaved during devaluation episodes, are equally important, both to inform the construction of the theoretical model and to act as a continuing test of the model's explanatory power.

This study summarizes research I have conducted in order to build up those stylized facts. It focuses on a narrow set of questions: How have key indicators of macroeconomic and external performance moved before, during, and after devaluations in developing countries? What are the obvious interrelationships among their movements? What *prima facie* evidence do these findings provide concerning the applicability of currently popular views about devaluations?

To answer these questions, my research exploits data for a set of 50 to 90 devaluations (depending on data availability) out of a sample of 107 devaluations imposed between 1953 and 1983. These episodes were all "maxi" devaluations: discrete changes in the nominal exchange rate with respect to the U.S. dollar of at least 15 percent within a few months. For each devaluation, I calculated the movements in a variety of indicators suggested by either theoretical considerations or policy concerns: the trade and payments balances, imports, exports, net capital flows, changes in reserves, inflation, the real exchange rate, and growth in gross domestic product (GDP). I calculated these movements for periods before and after devaluation for both the devaluing country and a control group comprising all the countries in the sample.

The plan of the study is as follows. Chapter 2 reviews the findings of earlier investigations of the devaluation process. Chapter 3 defines a stylized fact and outlines the methodology applied to the data. Chapter 4 describes the results. Chapter 5 discusses some preliminary work to test different explanations for the stylized trends indentified by the statistical analysis. Chapter 6 summarizes the major findings and points out potential directions for future research.

2 WHAT HAVE PREVIOUS STUDIES SHOWN?

Two empirical approaches have been followed to determine the effects of devaluations on external balance and macroeconomic performance. One examines changes in country performance at the time of devaluation. The other applies econometric methods to time series to determine the impact of exchange-rate changes on various performance variables (for examples of the second approach, see Khan, 1974; Goldstein, 1974; Miles, 1979; and Edwards, 1985). A third, somewhat less direct, approach to the problem uses simulation models or reduced-form equations to analyze exchange-rate equations (see Gylfasen and Risager, 1984, and Gylfasen and Schmid, 1983).

The following survey implicitly sets aside this large body of empirical research devoted not to devaluations per se but to the effects of exchange rates over time on imports, exports, and other indicators. While time-series analyses of exchange-rate effects may be entirely appropriate for certain purposes, there are important reasons why they are inappropriate for characterizing devaluation episodes. First and most obviously, they do not tell us what has happened historically during devaluation episodes. Real exchange rates move more or less continuously over time; they merely show more exceptional movement during devaluations. Second, not only are devaluations typically associated with other stabilization policies, but they are large, discrete events, and their influence, particularly as regards expectations, may differ qualitatively from slower, more routine exchange-rate adjustments. Finally, and this is true of most macroeconomic time-series analysis, it is very difficult to estimate equations relating target variables to the exchange rate in the absence of information about the lengths of the response lags involved. Proper specification of the structural relationship depends upon knowledge of the dynamic relationship; conversely, identifying the dynamics of response is difficult when the basic functional relationship is not well understood. Concentrating on devaluations may circumvent this problem, since there is more reason to presume that at the time of devaluation the economy is not responding to past changes in the nominal exchange rate.

As suggested in the Introduction, the inspiration for this research derives from the considerably older study of Cooper (1971a). Cooper examined 24 devaluations imposed by developing countries between 1959 and 1966, focusing on the changes in trade flows from the year before to the year after each devaluation. He found the trade balance (measured in foreign cur-

3

rency) to improve in 15 out of 24 cases, while even more cases showed improvement in the balance of payments (reserve accumulation). The trade-balance improvements derived from both increases in exports and decreases in imports, and these effects remained when allowance was made for changes in world demand (affecting exports) and changes in domestic output (affecting imports). Cooper also showed that while prices and wages tended to rise following devaluation, they did not rise by enough to offset fully the initial change in the nominal exchange rate. Finally, there were indications of contractionary tendencies following devaluation on the part of some elements of aggregate demand. In sum, Cooper's results were consistent with the most optimistic views regarding devaluation, except for his finding of some contractionary tendencies.

While Cooper attempted to control for changes in the international and domestic environment when measuring responses to devaluation, his focus on one-year changes was highly limiting. My own work shows vividly that macroeconomic and external-balance performance may deteriorate markedly prior to the devaluation, making it unclear whether any improvement observed immediately following devaluation is merely cyclical or results from the devaluation itself. To some extent, Bhagwat and Onitsuka (1974) dealt with this problem by comparing longer-term trends in exports and imports during devaluation episodes. While they found evidence of positive long-term export responses to devaluations, they found little indication of significant import responses. Presumably, these findings represented at least partial evidence of long-term improvement in the balance of trade.

But Bhagwat and Onitsuka did not focus directly on the two "bottom line" indicators of external performance: the balances of trade and payments. Salant (1976) examined the responses of these variables to 101 devaluations in both developed and developing countries, calculating their change from three years before to three years after each exchange-rate change. He found that the balance of trade improved in only 46 cases, while the balance of payments improved in 75. This evidence supports a frequently, if informally, made argument that devaluations help countries not by causing real adjustments but by stimulating capital inflows or reducing capital outflows.

Salant, however, did not control for changes in the international environment, and many of the devaluations he studied took place in the mid-1970s, a period of deteriorating trade balances but increased capital inflows for many countries. Hence, it is not clear that the measured performance of the devaluing economies differed significantly from that of the contemporaneous nondevaluing economies. Research by Donovan (1981) is helpful here. He focused on twelve IMF-sponsored devaluations between 1970 and 1976, comparing the performance of the devaluing economies with that of all

4

non–oil-exporting developing countries. He found that devaluations tend to improve export growth in the long run, though not initially, a result consistent with the "J-curve" view of export response. Paradoxically, he found that import growth rose following a devaluation, though by less than the eventual rise in export growth. Finally, while he found that the inflation rate rose, meaningful reductions in GDP growth were registered only for those programs specifically aimed at import restraint.

Recently, Edwards (1987) applied techniques similar to Donovan's to 18 Latin American devaluations. Edwards found that the current account and levels of international reserves initially deteriorated following the devaluations he studied but then improved over longer (three-year) horizons. Inflation rates tended to increase, while real exchange rates generally appreciated in the years following devaluation.

Gylfason (1987) also used a comparison-group approach in his study of IMF programs implemented during 1977-79. He found that countries with IMF programs that included devaluations showed improved balance-of-payments performance relative to a reference group of nonprogram countries experiencing payments imbalances, but differences in inflation and output growth were not statistically significant. Balance-of-payments improvements were also more marked among the devaluing countries than among IMF-program countries that did not devalue, but inflation performance was poorer and differences in output growth were not statistically significant.

To summarize, direct evidence concerning the impact of devaluations on external balance and macroeconomic performance is mixed and incomplete (see Bird, 1983, for a more detailed and comprehensive survey). There appears to be some consensus that devaluations are followed by improvements in capital inflows and the balance of payments. Only the earliest study, Cooper (1971a), finds movements in both imports and exports in the directions predicted by conventional trade theory. While both Bhagwat and Onitsuka (1974) and Donovan (1981) find some evidence of long-term improvement in exports, neither study shows any negative import response, and Salant (1976) finds an actual deterioration in long-term trade-balance performance. Edwards (1987) confirms the possibility of initial increases in trade and payments deficits, though these are shown to narrow thereafter. The evidence on macroeconomic performance is even sketchier. While Cooper, Donovan, Edwards, and Gylfason find evidence that inflation rises following devaluation, their results differ as to the response of real GDP growth.

3   RESEARCH METHODOLOGY

Before I describe my own strategy for defining the "stylized facts" of devaluation, it will be instructive to review the limitations of a simple empirical study of these events. The initial rough cut at the evidence should have a fairly modest goal: to characterize the historical responses of economies to devaluations of their currencies. While this goal is less ambitious than estimating the structural parameters of an economy's response to devaluation, we still want to exclude any systematic effects of factors that are clearly not associated with the devaluation itself.

The movement of an economic indicator during a devaluation episode can be thought of as deriving from four factors: (a) the exchange-rate change itself, (b) other policies of the stabilization program, (c) changes in the international or external environment, and (d) changes in exogenous domestic factors.

Eventually, we want to isolate the impact of the first factor, the exchange-rate change itself. A preliminary characterization of the devaluation process, however, might satisfactorily stop at isolating the combined effects of the first two factors, the devaluation-cum-stabilization program. It is nevertheless necessary to control for influential factors in the remaining two categories that are systematically related to the timing of devaluations, lest the stylized characterization of the devaluation process be biased. For example, if a country always devalued at the trough of its commodity-price cycle, its terms of trade would systematically rise following its devaluations. In consequence, the "stylized fact" one might infer from the country's data—that the dollar value of exports tends to rise following devaluation—might lead one erroneously to connect the export rebounds to the devaluations themselves. To jump ahead somewhat, my research at least partially accounts for this type of spurious correlation by comparing the devaluing country's performance with the performance of a control group of countries. However, I could find no fully satisfactory method of controlling for exogenous domestic events.

The data on external-balance and macroeconomic-performance indicators during devaluations were analyzed in three steps. These procedures are described in detail below, followed by a discussion of the data set. Briefly, the first step was to calculate the value of each indicator for each of the seven years spanning every devaluation episode for which the requisite data were available; the values of the indicator for each year were then averaged across all devaluation episodes to create an average time profile for that indicator. Second, an analogous profile was calculated for the average performance of that indicator for the entire country sample. Finally, a number of statistical tests were applied to discern whether the behavior of the devaluing economies differed significantly from the behavior of the entire sample during the same time periods.

Calculating the Time Profiles of Response

For each devaluation, the value of a particular indicator for the devaluing country was calculated for each of seven years, the three years preceding the devaluation and the four years following it. In general, these years did not coincide with the calendar years to which my annual data pertained. Accordingly, the indicator values were constructed as weighted averages of the appropriate calendar-year values with numbers of months as weights. For example, if a devaluation took place in July 1972, indicator values for the year immediately following (which is referred to as the "year of devaluation," or year T) were constructed by averaging the 1972 and 1973 values with weights of five-twelfths and seven-twelfths, respectively; values for the three years preceding and three years following that year were constructed analogously. The value of the indicator for each year was then averaged (unweighted) with the corresponding values for every other devaluation episode in the sample. The result is the average, or stylized, time profile for that indicator over the course of the typical devaluation episode. In aggregating across devaluations, both mean and median averages were calculated. In general, these moved together, though often at very different levels.

Averaging "raw" dollar figures for trade balances, imports, exports, and other variables would produce results unduly influenced by the performance of the largest economies. Therefore, level values of such variables were scaled, or divided by the value of nominal GDP during the year of the country's devaluation, before they were averaged with those of other countries. This procedure corrects for differences in economy size without allowing changes in the scaling factor to influence movements in the performance indicator. Growth rates and other key ratios were already scaled and therefore received no further processing.

Note that both very large and relatively small devaluations were averaged together in the statistical sample. Since large devaluations might be more influential than small ones, it would eventually be desirable to take their size into account. For this initial cut at the data, however, it was important to determine the broadest stylized characterization of economic performance during devaluation episodes. Such a characterization could be misleading if the smaller devaluations were of the more routine, crawling-peg variety, and the 15 percent cutoff used to select the devaluations was intended to exclude them.

Controlling for Sources of Spurious Correlation

As stated above, the time path of an indicator during a devaluation may be viewed as a response to four factors: the exchange-rate change itself, associated stabilization policies, exogenous international events, and exogenous domestic events. At the moment, I know of no straightforward, fully satisfactory way of controlling for the influence of exogenous domestic events systematically associated with the timing of devaluations. For example, countries may regularly devalue when near the bottom of a business cycle. As in the case of the commodity-price cycle discussed above, GDP growth would then tend systematically to improve after devaluations. There is no way to correct the resultant time profile of GDP growth for this spurious effect without a fully developed model explaining output growth. At the very least, however, inspection of the year-by-year time path of output would help to identify the problem; if such a pattern existed, it would show up as a fall in output growth in the period prior to devaluation. In fact, such deteriorations were evident for a number of indicators studied.

Fortunately, there are more promising ways to control for the influence of external or international factors systematically related to the timing of devaluations. Some authors (Bhagwat and Onitsuka, 1974, and Cooper, 1971a and 1971b) have attempted to control for fluctuations in international conditions by estimating the impact of these fluctuations on the devaluing country's exports; such effects were then removed from or compared with actual export changes. This approach depends excessively on the appropriateness of the prediction model used. Given our relative ignorance about the behavior of most key variables during devaluation episodes, confidence in such models, especially as applied to diverse countries, would appear optimistic at best.

Preferring to remain more agnostic about the causes of country external performance, I followed Donovan's (1981) lead and compared the performance of the devaluing country to the average performance of the entire sample during the time period corresponding to the devaluation episode. Hence, for a devaluation taking place, say, in Chile in 1971, median averages of indicator values for all countries in the sample were calculated for all (weighted averaged) years between 1968 and 1974. Chile's own performance profile during that period could then be compared with that of the comparison group to assess Chile's relative performance over the course of its devaluation episode. After the seven-year vectors of comparison-group averages were calculated, they were averaged across all devaluation episodes to construct control "time profiles" of performance indicators. That is, the median comparison-group averages corresponding to the first year of the seven-year devaluation period were averaged across all devaluations, the averages corresponding to the second year were averaged together, and so on. The resultant sets of seven cross-devaluation averages represent the stylized profiles of performance by the entire sample over the course of the devaluing country's devaluation episode. The deviations of the devaluing countries' profiles from the control-group profiles represent a stylized measure of the impact of the devaluations on the economies of the countries undergoing the experience.

Presumably, most swings in world demand, terms of trade, and international financing would be reflected in the experience and performance of the comparison group; no specific model of trade and payments determination is needed to control for international fluctuations. Note that the comparison group will always contain one or more devaluing countries. This feature was dictated by computational considerations, but it does not prejudice the results; rather, it imposes a conservative bias against identifying the results of devaluations because it makes the "treatment" and control groups more similar.

Tests for Statistical Significance

Tests for the significance of changes over time were conducted for each indicator for both the devaluing country's performance and the comparison group's performance, and for the difference between the two. In addition to testing for year-to-year changes in indicator values, three measures of longer-term change were tested. The basic long-run effect of devaluation was defined as the difference in the averages of indicator values between the first two years and the final three years of the devaluation episode. This excludes the years immediately preceding and immediately following the devaluation because my findings indicated that these years often differed markedly in character from the more stable ones before and after them. This longer-run measure was then decomposed into the difference between the preceding long-run period and the devaluation year (specifically, the twelve-month period following the month of devaluation) and the difference between the devaluation year and the average of the following three years.

Three different tests of the significance of performance changes over time were calculated. The first was a standard *t*-test of the mean of the differences in performance indicators (and longer-run averages) over time. (Note that this is not a test of the difference in mean averages for two periods, but rather a test to see if the mean of the sample of devaluation-specific changes between two periods is different from zero.) This test depends upon the normality of the vector of differences in data values, a condition not always

9

satisfied for some of the indicators. Accordingly, binomial-sign tests were also calculated for each change. In this test, the numbers of increases and decreases in a particular indicator across all devaluation episodes were totaled. Under the null hypothesis that the devaluations had no effect upon indicator performance, there would be a 0.5 probability of increase or decrease during any one episode. It was therefore possible to calculate the probability that the configuration of increases and decreases actually observed would have occurred under the null hypothesis. Although this test is reputed to be of low power, it frequently rejected the null hypothesis in the course of the study.

Both the t-test and the binomial-sign test rely on the median of comparison-group indicator values to represent fully the performance of the comparison group at a point in time. While the median average is considered superior to the mean when distributions are not symmetrical, it is not clear how well the median's movements reflect trends in the sample's performance. Ideally, for each devaluation we would like to know how changes in the devaluing country's performance compared with performance changes among nondevaluing countries at the same point in time.

An approach that responds well to this objective is the Wilcoxon rank-sum test for blocked data (see Lehmann, 1975, pp.134-137). For each devaluation, the change in indicator value associated with the devaluing country was included in the set of analogous values for the entire sample. The set was then arranged in ascending order of magnitude, and the relative rank of the devaluing country's value was recorded. Lehman (1975) shows that the expected mean and variance of the sum of these rank statistics across blocks of data (in this case, devaluation episodes) has an easily calculated normal approximation under the null hypothesis that devaluing-country and comparison-group performances do not differ. Accordingly, a t-test for this rank-sum statistic was calculated for every change (both yearly and longer-run) in the devaluing-country/comparison-group differential for every indicator. Its interpretation is exactly analogous to that of the more conventional t-test for the mean of differences also calculated for all changes in all indicator differentials.

The Data Set and Devaluation Sample

The data for almost all indicators studied were derived from the IMF's *International Financial Statistics* tape. Indicator definitions, line codes, and alternative sources are detailed in Appendix B. Appendix Table B-1 describes the devaluation sample, showing the devaluing country, the month and year of devaluation, the resultant quarterly change in the nominal exchange rate, and, for reference purposes, the preceding year's CPI inflation rate. These episodes represent discrete changes in the nominal exchange rate with respect to the dollar of at least 15 percent within three months. The 15 percent cutoff is somewhat arbitrary but represents an attempt to include as many "genuine" devaluations as possible while excluding more routine crawling-peg adjustments. The distribution of associated quarterly depreciation rates is displayed in Figure 1. It shows a fairly flat distribution of the depreciation rate to the immediate right of (higher than) the cutoff point. Hence, the devaluation sample apparently includes at least a substantial portion of the entire "universe" of devaluations.

Devaluations are typically associated with a variety of other, sometimes drastic policy actions; they are likely to differ qualitatively as well as quantitatively from a series of crawling-peg adjustments (see Krueger, 1978, for an extensive discussion of the economic, social, and political context sur-

FIGURE 1
DISTRIBUTION OF DEVALUATIONS BY SIZE OF NOMINAL DEPRECIATION

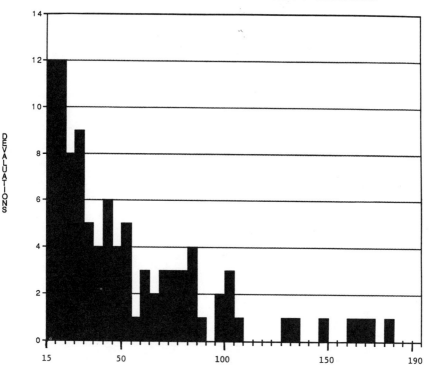

Percentage Nominal Depreciation

NOTE: Three depreciations over 200 percent were dropped from the sample.

rounding devaluations). With the increased attention paid in recent years to the crawling peg and other actively managed alternatives to fixed exchange rates, it might have been expected that maxi-devaluations would become less prominent policy choices. Such institutions as the IMF and World Bank would certainly prefer countries to regulate their exchange rates on a continuous basis. But, because they have failed to do so, the IMF and World Bank have continued to urge substantial devaluations to correct for past real appreciations. Figure 2 shows the number of devaluations in each year from 1953 to 1983. Far from becoming less prominent, devaluations have become increasingly frequent. What is more important, there are large variations in devaluation activity over time. An unusual number of devaluations took place in 1975, a period of widespread recession in the industrial world, and in 1982 and 1983, the peak of the debt crisis. This suggests, and the results described below clearly confirm, that the timing of devaluations was related systematically to periods of economic distress.

FIGURE 2
DISTRIBUTION OF DEVALUATIONS OVER TIME, 1953-83

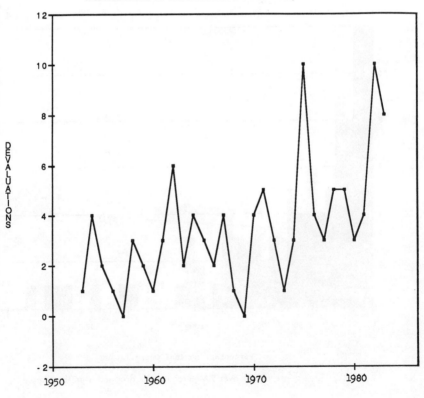

4   RESULTS

This survey of results is divided into three parts. First, the performance of the trade balance during devaluation episodes is described and decomposed into the contributing movements of imports and exports. Second, the financing of the trade and current-account balances is examined and decomposed into capital inflows and changes in reserves. Finally, two key measures of macroeconomic performance—inflation and output growth—are examined, as well as the corresponding movements of the real exchange rate.

Imports, Exports, and the Trade Balance

Conventional analyses of international trade and finance suggest that the successful devaluation will impact most heavily on the trade balance. An increase in the price of tradables relative to nontradables should increase the production of tradable goods and decrease their consumption, thus increasing exports, decreasing imports, and improving the trade balance (see Dornbusch, 1980). An improvement in the trade balance is also consistent with a more critical, "structuralist" view of devaluations, but here the improvement is thought to result less from enhanced export performance than from a contraction-induced decline in imports (see Krugman and Taylor, 1978).

In practice, the calculated response of the trade balance to a devaluation will depend on how the balance is measured. If imports and exports are measured on a volume or price-deflated basis, the trade balance should react to a devaluation as described above. If the flows are measured in domestic currency, the trade balance may follow a "J-curve" path. That is, the devaluation will automatically increase the domestic-currency value of any pre-existing deficit; this deficit will then shrink as export volume rises and import volume falls in response to relative price changes. Finally, the trade-balance response to a devaluation measured in foreign currency depends upon elasticities of export and import demand, as summarized in the Marshall-Lerner conditions. The developing countries are often modeled as small countries that cannot affect the world price of their exports; to the extent this is true, devaluations must always improve (or at least not injure) the trade balance. In fact, however, many developing countries produce large shares of the world supply of particular commodities, so that the response of their foreign-currency trade balances to devaluation is an open question.

13

The indicators described below are measured in U.S. dollars. For countries with balance-of-payments and external-debt problems, dollars are the most relevant measure to use. The movement of trade volumes would also be interesting, but these figures are available for substantially fewer devaluation cases. Nevertheless, such price data as were available were analyzed to shed some light on the movement of export and import volumes during devaluations.

The time profiles of the GDP-scaled trade balance over the devaluation period for the devaluing countries, for the entire comparison-group sample, and for the differences between the two measures are summarized in Table 1. Looking at the performance of the devaluing countries alone, it is apparent that the trade balance deteriorates steadily through the year immediately prior to devaluation (year $T-1$), improves or stabilizes for the subsequent two years (T and $T+1$), and then resumes its former deteriorating trend. (Recall that a value for year T represents the average value for the twelve-month period following the month of devaluation.) These movements are confirmed by both the parametric and binomial-sign tests, which show nearly significant rates of deterioration in $T-2$ and $T-1$ and improvement in T, followed by some further decline in $T+2$ and $T+3$.

Appendix Table A-1 summarizes the results of tests for longer-term changes in the trade balance. It shows that, notwithstanding the significant initial improvement in the trade balance following devaluation, the subsequent deterioration more than reverses this gain. Over the course of the entire period, the devaluing countries register an average deterioration of their trade balance. Hence, while there is some *prima facie* evidence that devaluation improves the trade balance in the short run, Salant's (1976) findings regarding the long-term impact of devaluations appear to be confirmed.

This finding is reversed, however, when the performance of the comparison group is taken into account. In Table 1, the average trade balance for the entire sample shows steady, continuous deterioration over the entire devaluation period. This does not necessarily indicate that these countries experienced secular declines in their trade balances, but rather that devaluations occurred most frequently during periods of widespread trade-balance deterioration. As a result, not only does the short-run ($T-1$ to $T+1$) impact of the devaluation become more pronounced, but the long-term change in the performance of the devaluing countries is seen to be positive relative to that of the entire sample (see the rank-sum t-statistic of 2.0 in the bottom left corner of Appendix Table A-1). Hence, the data suggest that devaluations are associated with absolute improvements in the trade balance in the short run and relatively slower rates of deterioration in the long run.

Imports. Having established the relative improvement in the trade bal-

14

TABLE 1

SUMMARY RESULTS FOR SCALED TRADE BALANCE

(*64 devaluations*)

	Year Relative to Devaluation Year T						
	T − 3	T − 2	T − 1	T	T + 1	T + 2	T + 3
Devaluing countries:							
Summary statistics:							
Mean	− 1.8	− 2.7	− 3.1	− 2.7	− 2.8	− 3.8	− 4.3
Median	− 1.2	− 1.6	− 1.9	− 1.5	− 1.7	− 2.5	− 2.8
Change from previous period:							
No. increasing		19	27	41	34	28	31
No. decreasing		45	37	23	30	36	33
Prob. if H_0 true		0.1	13	1.6	35.4	19.1	45.0
t-statistic		− 2.2	− 1.5	1.3	− 0.2	− 1.7	− 0.8
Total sample:							
Summary statistics:							
Mean	− 0.9	− 1.2	− 1.6	− 2.1	− 2.7	− 3.4	− 4.0
Median	− 0.8	− 1.1	− 1.4	− 1.4	− 1.7	− 2.5	− 3.4
Change from previous period:							
No. increasing		26	23	28	22	23	28
No. decreasing		38	41	36	42	41	36
Prob. if H_0 true		8.4	1.6	19.1	0.8	1.6	19.1
t-statistic		− 1.9	− 3.7	− 2.6	− 3.3	− 3.6	− 2.8
Difference:							
Summary statistics:							
Mean	− 0.9	− 1.5	− 1.5	− 0.6	− 0.1	− 0.5	− 0.3
Median	− 0.4	− 0.5	− 0.5	− 0.1	0.1	0.1	0.6
Change from previous period:							
No. increasing		28	30	41	40	31	31
No. decreasing		36	34	23	24	33	33
Prob. if H_0 true		19.1	35.4	1.6	3.0	4.5	4.5
t-statistic		− 1.8	− 0.1	2.7	0.8	− 0.6	0.4
Rank sum t-stat.		− 1.3	− 0.5	2.8	2.0	0.1	0.2

NOTE: Summary statistics and probabilities in percent.

ance experienced by the devaluing countries, we next determine whether the improvement resulted from increased exports or decreased imports. An examination of the levels of GDP-scaled imports during devaluation episodes revealed that, on average, they grew each year. This made it hard to discern any interesting patterns in their time profile. Table 2 summarizes

TABLE 2

SUMMARY RESULTS FOR IMPORT GROWTH

(*64 devaluations*)

	Year Relative to Devaluation Year T						
	T−3	T−2	T−1	T	T+1	T+2	T+3
Devaluing countries:							
Summary statistics:							
Mean	11.2	13.6	6.8	5.7	15.4	17.4	14.2
Median	10.0	8.8	5.6	4.5	11.1	13.7	9.1
Change from previous period:							
No. increasing		37	22	28	41	35	30
No. decreasing		27	42	36	23	29	34
Prob. if H_0 true		13.0	0.8	19.1	1.6	26.6	35.4
t-statistic		0.9	−3.1	−0.4	3.1	0.7	−0.8
Total sample:							
Summary statistics:							
Mean	9.7	13.7	14.3	13.1	14.5	14.5	10.9
Median	7.3	10.1	10.1	10.0	9.0	11.4	7.9
Change from previous period:							
No. increasing		48	37	36	39	39	28
No. decreasing		16	27	28	25	25	36
Prob. if H_0 true		0.0	13.0	19.1	5.2	5.2	19.1
t-statistic		2.4	0.4	−0.7	0.8	0.0	−1.7
Difference:							
Summary statistics:							
Mean	1.5	−0.1	−7.5	−7.4	0.1	2.8	3.3
Median	2.7	−1.3	−4.5	−5.5	2.0	2.3	1.2
Change from previous period:							
No. increasing		28	21	27	41	35	34
No. decreasing		36	43	37	23	29	30
Prob. if H_0 true		19.1	0.4	13.0	1.6	26.6	35.4
t-statistic		−0.8	−3.9	0.1	3.2	0.8	0.2
Rank sum t-stat.		−1.0	−3.6	−0.2	3.3	1.4	0.1

NOTE: Summary statistics and probabilities in percent.

the profile of the growth of dollar-value imports over time. It indicates a pattern of import behavior very much at variance with either conventional or structuralist predictions for import movements during devaluation episodes. While the entire sample shows approximately steady growth in imports over time, import growth in the devaluing countries falls off significantly in the year preceding devaluation, deteriorates slightly more in the

16

year just following devaluation, and then turns up significantly in the year T + 1. Appendix Table A-2 indicates mild evidence of long-run increases in import growth relative to the entire sample; this is decomposed into highly significant decreases in relative growth rates up to the year of devaluation, followed by highly significant increases thereafter.

Finally, the accompanying table summarizes the movement of foreign-currency (dollar) import prices during devaluation episodes. Owing to the small number of observations (25) and of comparison countries (15), only the basic calculations for the devaluing economies are presented. They indicate much lower variation in the growth of import prices than is observed in the growth of import dollar values. Moreover, during the year immediately preceding devaluation, when import-value growth is shown to fall markedly, import-price growth apparently rises. This suggests that import-volume growth may vary even more substantially than is implied by the import-value data.

SUMMARY RESULTS FOR IMPORT-PRICE GROWTH
(25 *devaluations; in percent*)

	Year Relative to Devaluation Year T						
	T − 3	T − 2	T − 1	T	T + 1	T + 2	T + 3
Mean	7	7	8	6	8	8	8
Median	3	3	7	3	4	2	2

Exports. Turning to Table 3, we note that, as with imports, export growth falls markedly in the year before devaluation. Unlike imports, which continue to fall (in growth terms) in the subsequent year, export growth rises to approximate parity with comparison-group performance in the first year following devaluation and increases in the following year as well. These results hold both absolutely and relative to the control group. As Appendix Table A-3 indicates, the devaluing countries also show marked long-term increases in export growth relative to the entire sample. It should be noted in Table 3, though, that by T + 3 the median growth-rate differential returns to about the T − 3 value.

The very fast positive response of exports to devaluation observed in the data appears to contradict the presumption of "short-term elasticity pessimism" to be found in much of the literature. While structuralists will generally concede that in the long run depreciations of the real exchange rate will improve export performance, most analysts of the "get the prices right" school will concede the existence of short-term export inelasticities. By contrast, the results presented here indicate that at least half the longer-term

17

TABLE 3

SUMMARY RESULTS FOR EXPORT GROWTH

(64 devaluations)

	T−3	T−2	T−1	T	T+1	T+2	T+3
				Year Relative to Devaluation Year T			
Devaluing countries:							
Summary statistics:							
Mean	11.0	10.9	5.8	13.4	19.9	15.9	14.6
Median	8.5	8.2	3.8	12.8	16.7	13.2	8.2
Change from previous period:							
No. increasing		30	25	43	42	31	30
No. decreasing		34	39	21	22	33	34
Prob. if H_0 true		35.4	5.2	0.4	0.8	45.0	35.4
t-statistic		−0.0	−2.2	3.2	2.3	−1.2	−0.5
Total sample:							
Summary statistics:							
Mean	10.5	11.7	10.9	11.9	13.0	11.0	8.0
Median	7.3	8.6	8.2	9.4	9.6	9.2	6.2
Change from previous period:							
No. increasing		36	30	41	39	28	28
No. decreasing		28	34	23	25	36	36
Prob. if H_0 true		19.1	35.4	1.6	5.2	19.1	19.1
t-statistic		1.3	−0.9	0.9	0.9	−1.7	−2.3
Difference:							
Summary statistics:							
Mean	0.4	−0.8	−5.0	1.5	6.9	5.0	6.7
Median	1.2	−0.4	−4.4	3.5	7.0	4.0	2.0
Change from previous period:							
No. increasing		27	21	45	39	31	37
No. decreasing		37	43	19	25	33	27
Prob. if H_0 true		13.0	0.4	0.1	5.2	45.0	13.0
t-statistic		−0.6	−2.0	3.4	2.1	−0.8	0.8
Rank sum t-stat.		−1.1	−2.1	3.4	2.0	−0.5	0.4

NOTE: Summary statistics and probabilities in percent.

increase in export growth occurs in the first year following devaluation; after further improvement in the subsequent year, export growth shows mild deterioration.

The short-term export-growth response is strong enough to suggest that the calculations may be picking up the effects of changes in external conditions. Yet all world-demand and terms-of-trade changes should be reflected in movements of comparison-group export performance, and this performance is virtually stable throughout the devaluation period. The explanation may be that countries devalue in response to declines in the prices of the commodities they export exclusively (or that are not widely produced in the sample group). Cyclical upswings in these country-specific commodity prices might then induce upswings in export growth that are incorrectly attributed to the preceding devaluations. This cycle in prices and exports would not be reflected in the performance of the comparison group.

To test this possibility, the export unit values of the devaluing countries were compared with those of the comparison group. As Table 4 indicates, the variation in the growth of export prices is much smaller than, and cannot explain, the variation in the growth of export value during devaluations. There is no statistically significant drop in the growth of export prices in the year before devaluation. For the year immediately following, the binomial-sign tests do support an increase in export-price growth, but this is confirmed by neither the t-test nor the rank-sum test. Hence, both the pre-devaluation fall and post-devaluation rise in exports occurred on a volume as well as a value basis and cannot be attributed to movements in export prices alone. As indicated in Appendix Table A-4, there is no evidence of long-term movements in export-price growth either.

Finally, it should be noted that these data measure export transactions, not export production. Large swings in recorded exports may reflect changes in the output of the exportable sector, but they may also reflect changes in export inventories, sales reporting, or the domestic consumption of exportables.

Summary. This analysis suggests that the reduction in trade deficits found to follow devaluations may be attributable to increases in export activity rather than decreases in imports. In the year prior to devaluation, both export and import growth fall, with the net result that the trade deficit widens. In the year following devaluation, import growth falls only marginally but export growth rises dramatically. Export levels rise relative to imports, and the trade deficit shrinks. In the year after that, import growth rises markedly, but the continued expansion of exports maintains the improvement in the trade balance.

Because movements in the trade balance are determined by changes in the levels of exports and imports rather than by changes in their growth rates, the table on page 21 below is presented to decompose trade-balance movements after devaluation (year T) into the four possible responses of exports and imports. While in fourteen cases where the trade balance showed improvement imports actually rose, only two trade-balance improvements occurred when exports fell. Alternatively, no trade-balance deteriorations

19

TABLE 4

SUMMARY RESULTS FOR EXPORT-PRICE GROWTH

(51 devaluations)

	Year Relative to Devaluation Year T						
	T−3	T−2	T−1	T	T+1	T+2	T+3
Devaluing countries:							
Summary statistics:							
Mean	6.5	5.2	5.7	8.1	8.2	4.4	5.8
Median	4.2	1.7	0.5	4.3	4.7	4.3	1.7
Change from previous period:							
No. increasing		26	27	33	25	22	30
No. decreasing		25	24	18	26	29	21
Prob. if H_0 true		50.0	39.0	2.4	50.0	20.1	13.1
t-statistic		−0.4	0.1	0.7	0.0	−1.3	0.4
Total sample:							
Summary statistics:							
Mean	5.6	6.3	5.0	5.1	6.7	6.0	4.1
Median	1.7	2.4	2.2	2.9	3.5	3.0	1.2
Change from previous period:							
No. increasing		32	24	27	29	20	22
No. decreasing		19	27	24	22	31	29
Prob. if H_0 true		4.6	39.0	39.0	20.1	8.0	20.1
t-statistic		0.5	−1.0	0.1	1.3	−0.5	−1.3
Difference:							
Summary statistics:							
Mean	0.8	−1.1	0.7	3.0	1.5	−1.7	1.6
Median	2.5	−0.7	−1.7	1.4	1.1	1.3	0.5
Change from previous period:							
No. increasing		22	26	32	24	24	26
No. decreasing		29	25	19	27	27	25
Prob. if H_0 true		20.1	50.0	4.6	39.0	39.0	50.0
t-statistic		−0.9	0.7	0.8	−0.5	−1.3	1.5
Rank sum t-stat.		−1.1	0.6	1.5	−1.2	−0.7	1.2

NOTE: Summary statistics and probabilities in percent.

occurred when imports fell. Given the strong impetus of exports, a decline in imports was a sufficient but by no means necessary condition for a rise in the trade balance. These findings appear to contradict the widespread contention that devaluations improve the trade balance in the short term by reducing imports, not by inducing greater exports.

DECOMPOSITION OF TRADE-BALANCE MOVEMENTS FOLLOWING DEVALUATION
(*number of cases*)

	Exports Rise, Imports Rise	Exports Rise, Imports Fall	Exports Fall, Imports Rise	Exports Fall, Imports Fall
Trade balance rises	14	24	0	2
Trade balance falls	16	0	7	0
Total	30	24	7	2

The Financing of the External Deficit

As we saw in Chapter 2, there appears to be agreement that even if the balance of trade continues to deteriorate after devaluation, the balance of payments should improve. Generally, the balance of payments is defined as some variant of the change in holdings of international reserves. Devaluations are deemed to enhance net capital inflows and hence (for a given current account) enhance the accumulation of reserves. The monetary approach to the balance of payments predicts that devaluations will raise domestic price levels, reduce real balances, and hence create an excess demand for money that will act to induce inflows of reserves (see Connolly and Taylor, 1976, and Rabin and Yeager, 1982). An alternative explanation focuses on the behavior of commercial banks and international financial institutions, which are presumed to withhold or ration credit to developing-country governments until they take some action, such as a devaluation, to correct their external-balance problems. In her survey of the National Bureau of Economic Research project on foreign-trade regimes, Krueger (1978) suggests that this behavior may be an important factor explaining variations in capital flows into many devaluing countries. Finally, another approach highlights speculative reversals or moderations of capital flight as an explanation of improvements in the balance of payments following devaluation. In such analyses (see Krugman, 1979), expectations of future devaluations motivate capital outflows before the exchange rate changes. After devaluation, these outflows cease, and—depending upon other policies followed by the monetary authorities—net capital inflows may occur.

It should be noted that evidence of increased accumulation of reserves can be used to confirm these hypotheses only if current-account balances deteriorate subsequent to devaluation. Otherwise, improved reserves positions may merely reflect improved current-account performance. In fact, the performance of the current account during devaluation episodes closely matches that of the trade balance. The data indicate that, both in absolute terms and relative to the entire sample, the current account deteriorates prior to devaluation before improving in the two years following the event. As with the trade balance, the current account then begins to fall off again but registers long-term improvement relative to the entire sample profile. Hence, we must study capital inflows themselves to evaluate the hypotheses discussed here.

Capital Inflows. Table 5 indicates that the time pattern of net capital inflows is very similar to that of the trade and current-account deficits. It rises steadily from $T-3$ to $T-1$, just as the current account does, and it also appears to rise unambiguously in the years $T+2$ and $T+3$. During years T and $T+1$, however, capital inflows show some evidence of falling, or at least stabilizing. Hence, there is little evidence that the effect of the devaluations is to increase capital inflows, though some longer-term effects may work in this direction. Appendix Table A-5 indicates that, for the devaluing countries alone, capital inflows rise unambiguously over the full course of the devaluation period.

The presumption that devaluations enhance net capital inflows in the long run is contradicted strongly, however, when the performance of the comparison group is taken into account. Net capital inflows grow steadily for this group over the entire devaluation period. From $T-1$ to $T+1$, the evidence indicates that growth in capital inflows is much lower in the devaluing countries than in the entire sample; the tests summarized in Appendix Table A-5 indicate that in the long run growth in capital inflows is clearly higher for the total sample.

The failure of net capital inflows to rise in response to devaluation appears to contradict all three of the views sketched at the beginning of this section. A number of potential reconciliations of this contradiction merit further investigation.

First, no attempt is made to distinguish accommodating from nonaccommodating capital flows. Prior to devaluation, widening trade deficits may be financed by suppliers' credits and delays in payments, which boost capital inflows above the level dictated by voluntary portfolio choices alone. Following devaluation, improved trade balances may reduce the importance of these credits and lower net capital inflows below the level they might otherwise reach. Thus, a fall in accommodating capital inflows from before to after devaluation could mask increases in nonaccommodating flows occurring at the same time.

Second, while many devaluations in the sample were accompanied by IMF credits or other external-finance programs, this was not true for all of them. Moreover, in many instances devaluations followed earlier unsuccessful programs that were also accompanied by extensions of external credit. In the future, researchers should distinguish between public and private credit when analyzing the behavior of capital flows during devalua-

TABLE 5

Summary Results for Scaled Capital Inflows

(62 *devaluations*)

| | \multicolumn{7}{c}{Year Relative to Devaluation Year T} | | | | | | |
	T−3	T−2	T−1	T	T+1	T+2	T+3
Devaluing countries:							
Summary statistics:							
Mean	2.5	3.2	3.5	3.5	3.8	4.7	5.8
Median	2.0	2.7	2.6	2.7	2.8	2.9	4.5
Change from previous period:							
No. increasing		41	37	30	33	39	38
No. decreasing		21	25	32	29	23	24
Prob. if H_0 true		0.8	8.1	45.0	35.2	2.8	4.9
t-statistic		1.9	1.1	−0.2	0.8	2.4	2.1
Total sample:							
Summary statistics:							
Mean	1.6	2.0	2.5	3.0	3.5	4.2	4.9
Median	1.9	2.3	2.5	3.1	3.7	5.0	5.4
Change from previous period:							
No. increasing		47	45	44	47	48	44
No. decreasing		15	17	18	15	14	18
Prob. if H_0 true		0.0	0.0	0.1	0.0	0.0	0.1
t-statistic		5.4	7.0	5.1	4.8	5.5	4.6
Difference:							
Summary statistics:							
Mean	0.9	1.2	1.1	0.5	0.3	0.5	0.9
Median	0.0	0.4	0.1	−0.4	−0.8	−2.1	−0.9
Change from previous period:							
No. increasing		36	30	24	24	33	35
No. decreasing		26	32	38	38	29	27
Prob. if H_0 true		12.6	45.0	4.9	4.9	35.2	18.7
t-statistic		0.9	−0.5	−1.5	−0.4	0.4	0.7
Rank sum t-stat.		1.1	−0.8	−1.7	−1.6	−0.0	1.0

NOTE: Summary statistics and probabilities in percent.

tions; they should also distinguish devaluations associated with IMF programs from those that were independently administered.

Finally, the failure of net capital inflows to fall prior to devaluation and to rise thereafter, as predicted by analyses of capital flight and speculative attacks, may reflect differences between the assumptions of these models and the historical context of many devaluations. Given the presence of extensive exchange and capital controls, much capital flight prior to devaluation may have been contained or, as is more likely, gone unrecorded. The reversal of capital flight after devaluation, moreover, depends upon the ability of the authorities to stabilize the economy, a condition not satisfied in many instances (see Edwards, 1987).

Reserves Flows. Table 6 and Appendix Table A-6 summarize evidence that strongly confirms the presumption that devaluations improve the balance of payments, if not for the reasons generally cited. Outflows of reserves increase to their highest point in the year directly preceding devaluation. This is not surprising in view of the fact that the current account reaches its pre-devaluation nadir in that year. Subsequently, the performance of reserves improves markedly. Hence, the long-run performance of reserves in the devaluing countries shows substantial improvement over the pre-devaluation performance.

The entire sample also shows an increase in accumulation of reserves in the year following devaluation, but the significant differences between devaluing-country and comparison-group performance in years T and T + 1 indicate that the improvement in the balance of payments was more marked among the devaluing countries. Compared with the comparison group, the devaluing countries also showed significant long-term improvement in reserves accumulation, concentrated especially in the years directly following the devaluation itself (see Appendix Table A-6).

Very much related to the rate of reserves accumulation is its scaled level-form equivalent, the reserves/imports ratio. Expressed in terms of months of imports, this reserves figure is of special interest to countries facing severe balance-of-payments difficulties. The calculated time pattern of the reserves/imports ratio closely follows that of the rate of reserves accumulation. It steadily declines prior to devaluation and reaches its lowest point in the year immediately preceding it. Two years of improvement follow immediately after devaluation, and then the ratio appears to stabilize. In absolute terms, the evidence of long-term improvement in the reserves ratio is fairly ambiguous, but the data do support a long-term improvement in devaluing-country reserves positions relative to the comparison group.

Summary. Does the balance of payments improve by more than the trade balance? As the table on page 26 makes clear, in the short run the improvement in the trade and current-account balances is clearly the cause of the improvement in the balance of payments, given virtually stable capital inflows. Between the year before and the year after the devaluation, the balances of trade and payments exhibited marked and very similar patterns of improvement, while about equal numbers of countries experienced increases and decreases in their net capital inflows.

24

TABLE 6

SUMMARY RESULTS FOR SCALED RESERVES OUTFLOWS

(65 *devaluations*)

	T−3	T−2	T−1	T	T+1	T+2	T+3
			Year Relative to Devaluation Year T				
Devaluing countries:							
Summary statistics:							
Mean	−0.0	0.1	0.3	−0.2	−0.9	−0.3	−0.5
Median	−0.1	0.1	0.2	0.1	−0.2	−0.1	−0.1
Change from previous period:							
No. increasing		33	33	20	22	31	28
No. decreasing		32	32	45	43	34	37
Prob. if H_0 true		50.0	50.0	0.1	0.6	40.2	16.1
t-statistic		0.7	0.7	−2.8	−2.4	1.4	−0.8
Total sample:							
Summary statistics:							
Mean	−0.2	−0.2	−0.2	−0.4	−0.4	−0.2	−0.1
Median	−0.2	−0.1	−0.2	−0.3	−0.3	−0.1	−0.1
Change from previous period:							
No. increasing		32	29	19	27	35	31
No. decreasing		33	36	46	38	30	34
Prob. if H_0 true		50.0	22.9	0.1	10.7	31.0	40.2
t-statistic		−0.1	−0.4	−2.9	−0.3	1.7	1.4
Difference:							
Summary statistics:							
Mean	0.2	0.3	0.5	0.1	−0.5	−0.1	−0.4
Median	0.1	0.3	0.4	0.4	0.1	−0.0	−0.0
Change from previous period:							
No. increasing		34	37	26	24	33	28
No. decreasing		31	28	39	41	32	37
Prob. if H_0 true		40.2	16.1	6.8	2.3	50.0	16.1
t-statistic		0.8	0.8	−1.9	−2.3	1.1	−1.4
Rank sum t-stat.		1.2	1.2	−1.7	−2.6	−0.0	−0.7

NOTE: Summary statistics and probabilities in percent.

In the long run, by contrast, most devaluing countries suffered trade-balance deterioration coupled with improved balance-of-payments performance. This reflected the fact that net capital inflows grew more quickly than the current-account balance deteriorated.

However, both the balance of trade and the balance of payments im-

TRADE AND PAYMENTS PERFORMANCE OF THE DEVALUING COUNTRIES
AND RELATIVE TO THE COMPARISON GROUP
(*number of cases*)

	Improvement	Deterioration
Performance:		
Short run:		
Trade balance	41	23
Payments balance	45	20
Long run:		
Trade balance	25	39
Payments balance	46	19
Performance relative to sample:		
Short run:		
Trade balance	41	23
Payments balance	39	26
Long run:		
Trade balance	38	26
Payments balance	43	22

proved for the devaluing countries relative to the comparison group in the long run. While devaluing-country capital inflows grew more slowly then did those of the comparison group, their trade balances deteriorated more slowly as well. The accompanying table indicates that, relative to the comparison group, short- and long-run performances were roughly comparable.

Prices and the Real Exchange Rate

There is substantial agreement that a devaluation, by raising the local-currency prices of some portion of both final and intermediate goods, will raise the price level. Because it takes time for this increase to work its way through the economy's price structure, however, there is also widespread, if not universal, agreement that a devaluation will result in at least a temporary increase in the inflation rate (see Krueger, 1978, for a dissenting opinion). Two related issues are more controversial. First, a devaluation may lead to an initial bout of inflation that becomes incorporated into expectations; as a result, it could take a long time for the inflation rate to decline to its pre-devaluation level. Second, a nominal devaluation may raise the domestic price level to the same extent, completely nullifying any real-exchange-rate depreciation. Both these issues will be examined in the light of evidence presented below.

CPI Inflation. Table 7 shows clearly that the rate of consumer-price infla-

TABLE 7

SUMMARY RESULTS FOR CPI GROWTH

(74 devaluations)

	T−3	T−2	T−1	T	T+1	T+2	T+3
				Year Relative to Devaluation Year T			
Devaluing countries:							
Summary statistics:							
Mean	16.2	15.4	19.0	27.9	28.8	26.0	25.7
Median	9.9	11.2	14.0	17.3	14.7	11.5	13.9
Change from previous period:							
No. increasing		48	47	53	31	31	41
No. decreasing		26	27	21	43	43	33
Prob. if H_0 true		0.7	1.3	0.0	10.0	10.0	20.8
t-statistic		−0.2	1.2	2.2	0.2	−1.0	−0.1
Total sample:							
Summary statistics:							
Mean	7.4	8.2	8.8	8.7	9.5	10.3	10.8
Median	5.3	4.9	4.8	5.5	8.6	11.5	12.2
Change from previous period:							
No. increasing		40	42	43	49	48	39
No. decreasing		34	32	31	25	26	35
Prob. if H_0 true		28.1	14.8	10.0	0.4	0.7	36.4
t-statistic		2.0	1.6	−0.1	2.0	2.7	1.1
Difference:							
Summary statistics:							
Mean	8.8	7.2	10.2	19.2	19.3	15.7	14.9
Median	4.6	6.3	9.1	11.8	6.1	0.0	1.8
Change from previous period:							
No. increasing		41	46	51	26	23	39
No. decreasing		33	28	23	48	51	35
Prob. if H_0 true		20.8	2.4	0.1	0.7	0.1	36.4
t-statistic		−0.5	1.1	2.2	0.0	−1.3	−0.2
Rank sum t-stat.		0.9	3.1	4.4	−2.9	−3.7	−0.1

NOTE: Summary statistics and probabilities in percent.

tion rises markedly following devaluation. This is particularly true of the mean calculation and the test based on the mean. The median calculation indicates an acceleration of inflation in the year before devaluation, with continued increases in the following year. The inflation rates for the entire sample show steady but substantial increases across the devaluation period.

In consequence, the parametric *t*-statistic for the difference between devaluing-country and comparison-group performance shows significant relative increases in devaluing-country inflation in year T, while both the binomial-sign tests and rank-sum statistics indicate that the divergence begins in the preceding year. As regards this latter finding, it is often the case that prior to a devaluation an economy is increasingly beset by import shortages. Thus it is very possible that the prices of imported goods, and hence of consumer prices generally, will rise even before any official exchange-rate adjustment (see Krueger, 1978).

The more important issue is not whether inflation at first increases after devaluation but whether or not it subsequently falls. Looking at the devaluing countries alone, we can see mixed evidence that inflation rates do return to lower levels. Both the mean and median inflation rates are lower at T+3 than at T, though not by a great deal. In Appendix Table A-7, 36 devaluations show increases in inflation subsequent to the first year after devaluation and 38 show decreases.

This evidence, though weak, is more compelling when compared with that for the comparison group. While inflation rates among the devaluing countries stay approximately stable in the second half of the devaluation period, comparison-group inflation rates show continued, significant growth. Thus, the median inflation rate for the entire sample catches up to that of the devaluing countries by T+3, while the mean differential shows signs of eventual, if slow, convergence. Appendix Table A-7 indicates that, compared with the total sample, devaluing-country inflation accelerated through the year immediately following devaluation, after which it registered a relative decline. When we look at the relative movement of inflation over the entire devaluation period, only the binomial-sign test supports the contention that the rate of inflation in devaluing countries was increased in the long run. The most straightforward explanation for the devaluing countries' relatively stable inflation performance following their devaluations is that it represents the confounding of two offsetting factors: (a) the decline in inflation after its initial impetus from the devaluation and (b) the other on-going factors that were responsible for rising inflation rates throughout the developing countries.

The Real Exchange Rate. Whether or not inflation stabilizes, do price rises engendered by a devaluation completely reverse the impact of the initial real-exchange-rate depreciation? Because all countries in this sample experienced steady inflation during most of the period, the mere erosion of the devaluing country's real exchange rate does not prove this contention. Rather, the question is: Can a devaluation cause enough additional inflation to completely reverse the devaluation's real effects, forcing the real ex-

28

change rate to the same level it would have reached in the absence of devaluation?

One way to examine this issue is to compare the behavior of the two groups' real exchange rates over time.[1] This comparison is complicated by the fact that a number of countries experienced several devaluations in rapid succession, but this was not true for most of the sample. Table 8 indicates that between $T-1$, the year just before devaluation, and $T+3$, the real exchange rates of the devaluing countries appreciated by less than those of the comparison group.[2] Appendix Table A-8 confirms that over the long term the devaluing countries experienced a relative depreciation of their real exchange rates. If the real-exchange-rate depreciation of the devaluing countries was entirely eroded by the additional price increases resulting from devaluation, their real-exchange-rate differential with the comparison group should have eroded as well. This does not appear to have occurred. Accordingly, there is no evidence here to support the fear that countries will be unable to change their real exchange rates.

Do Devaluations Cause Contractions?

Criticisms of devaluation policy expressed frequently in the literature are based largely on the contention that devaluations are contractionary (see Diaz-Alejandro, 1965; Cooper, 1971a and 1971b; and Krugman and Taylor, 1978). Table 9 demonstrates that on average the environment for the devaluing countries was one of poor growth in real output. Over the devaluation period, the total sample suffered a significant decline in output growth (see Appendix Table A-9). The growth performance of the devaluing countries exhibits a by now familiar pattern: deterioration in growth rates—absolutely and relative to the comparison group—before the devaluation, and improved performance afterward. Note, first, that the growth rate never falls below 3 percent; a contraction, in the sense of actual decline in output levels, is not typical of most devaluations.

Second, a sharp and significant decline in output growth is registered by the devaluing countries, but it occurs in the year *preceding* the devaluation. This lower rate appears to be maintained virtually unchanged through the year following devaluation.

Finally, Appendix Table A-9 provides some evidence that growth in subsequent years turns upward in absolute terms and stronger evidence that growth improves relative to the comparison group. Hence, over the course

[1] The real exchange rate is defined here as the nominal exchange rate divided by the country's CPI.

[2] The calculations were actually performed on real-exchange-rate indexes, with 1975 equal to 1.

TABLE 8

SUMMARY RESULTS FOR REAL EXCHANGE RATES

(72 *devaluations*)

				Year Relative to Devaluation Year T			
	T−3	T−2	T−1	T	T+1	T+2	T+3
Devaluing countries:							
Summary statistics:							
Mean	1.34	1.26	1.26	1.41	1.37	1.30	1.24
Median	1.30	1.16	1.15	1.31	1.35	1.26	1.10
Change from previous period:							
No. increasing		8	32	53	21	17	20
No. decreasing		64	40	19	51	55	52
Prob. if H_0 true		0.0	20.5	0.0	0.0	0.0	0.0
t-statistic		−3.2	−0.2	6.1	−2.2	−3.6	−3.5
Total sample:							
Summary statistics:							
Mean	1.52	1.46	1.41	1.36	1.30	1.24	1.20
Median	1.66	1.64	1.58	1.56	1.44	1.21	1.06
Change from previous period:							
No. increasing		21	16	15	9	17	21
No. decreasing		51	56	57	63	55	51
Prob. if H_0 true		0.0	0.0	0.0	0.0	0.0	0.0
t-statistic		−5.2	−7.1	−7.1	−8.7	−7.1	−5.8
Difference:							
Summary statistics:							
Mean	−0.17	−0.20	−0.15	0.05	0.07	0.05	0.04
Median	−0.36	−0.48	−0.44	−0.25	−0.10	0.04	0.04
Change from previous period:							
No. increasing		14	45	66	38	23	33
No. decreasing		58	27	6	34	49	39
Prob. if H_0 true		0.0	2.2	0.0	36.2	0.1	27.8
t-statistic		−1.3	3.0	8.4	0.9	−0.9	−0.7
Rank sum *t*-stat.		−2.3	4.2	9.8	1.2	−2.4	−0.8

NOTE: Probabilities in percent.

of the entire devaluation period, the behavior of the two groups is comparable. This is the result of significant relative deterioration on the part of the devaluing countries up to the year of devaluation, followed by relative improvement thereafter. In sum, there is little evidence that devaluations are followed by significant contractions in output; recessions prior to deval-

TABLE 9

SUMMARY RESULTS FOR REAL GDP GROWTH

(*60 devaluations*)

	Year Relative to Devaluation Year T						
	T−3	T−2	T−1	T	T+1	T+2	T+3
Devaluing countries:							
Summary statistics:							
Mean	5.2	5.0	3.3	3.5	4.4	4.5	4.4
Median	4.7	4.9	3.9	3.5	5.2	4.6	5.5
Change from previous period:							
No. increasing		27	20	29	30	28	27
No. decreasing		33	40	31	30	32	33
Prob. if H_0 true		25.9	0.7	44.9	55.1	34.9	25.9
t-statistic		−0.2	−3.0	0.4	1.4	0.0	−0.2
Total sample:							
Summary statistics:							
Mean	5.2	5.2	5.0	5.0	5.0	4.9	4.5
Median	5.3	5.2	5.0	5.1	5.0	5.2	4.9
Change from previous period:							
No. increasing		34	27	33	37	31	23
No. decreasing		26	33	27	23	29	37
Prob. if H_0 true		18.3	25.9	25.9	4.6	44.9	4.6
t-statistic		0.2	−1.8	−0.3	0.1	−0.8	−2.8
Difference:							
Summary statistics:							
Mean	−0.0	−0.2	−1.7	−1.5	−0.5	−0.4	−0.1
Median	−0.6	−0.3	−1.1	−1.6	0.1	−0.7	0.7
Change from previous period:							
No. increasing		28	20	33	35	31	30
No. decreasing		32	40	27	25	29	30
Prob. if H_0 true		34.9	0.7	25.9	12.3	44.9	55.1
t-statistic		−0.3	−2.7	0.5	1.4	0.2	0.5
Rank sum t-stat.		−0.0	−2.4	−0.0	0.5	0.7	1.2

NOTE: Summary statistics and probabilities in percent.

uation appear to be more typical of the devaluation process. An extension of this research might examine more closely the movement of individual components of aggregate demand.

5 ACCOUNTING FOR THE STYLIZED FACTS
OF DEVALUATION

The stylized facts developed in Chapter 4 can be summarized to characterize the devaluation process. In the one- or two-year period immediately preceding a devaluation, the devaluing country experiences marked deterioration in the growth of its exports, imports, and real GDP, as well as in its reserves position. Immediately following the devaluation, export growth tends to rise sharply and the reserves position improves. Import growth continues to fall, though at a slower rate, and output growth remains about stable. Subsequently, export growth rises somewhat more before stabilizing, import growth rebounds to surpass pre-devaluation rates, and output growth slowly rises to match its earlier performance. In the course of the post-devaluation period, the initially improved trade balance and reserves position eventually resume their earlier deterioration, but at considerably slower rates than before.

This streamlined, in fact skeletal, characterization of the devaluation process raises far more questions than it answers. First, why do all the major performance indicators—exports, imports, output, and international reserves—show such sharp deterioration prior to the devaluation? Second, why do exports show such an unexpectedly pronounced response in the first year following devaluation, contradicting conventional views of the dynamics of export response? And, finally, what accounts for the sharp surge in imports and slow upswing in output growth observed in the subsequent period? Above all, the findings indicate that the proper focus of investigation should not be the impact of devaluations per se but rather the behavior of key performance indicators over the course of devaluation episodes.

Two basic scenarios come to mind that may explain these stylized trends. The first might be called the "Keynesian/neoclassical" scenario in that relative-price and expenditure effects share center stage. The driving factor is the real exchange rate, which before the devaluation appreciates rapidly in the face of accelerating domestic inflation. This reduces export growth and, through conventional multiplier effects, reduces output growth as well. The decline in output performance in turn offsets the effect of the appreciating real exchange rate enough to reduce import growth. After the devaluation, export growth resumes strongly, while output and import growth respond slowly and with lags. The trade balance and accumulation of reserves improve until imports rise and catch up with exports. Part of the lag in the resumption of import growth comes from the effect of the devaluation on relative prices. By the second year after the devaluation, this effect is considerably eroded, further encouraging import growth at about the time output growth resumes.

A second explanation for the trends observed during devaluation episodes might be called the "reserves constraint" scenario. Since this model does not address the causes of export behavior, we may assume, as above, that export behavior is driven by the real exchange rate. Exports fall prior to devaluation, and foreign-exchange revenues fall as well. The widening trade deficit is not fully accommodated by capital inflows, nor can it be fully financed by limited international reserves; in consequence, import rationing is imposed to stem the outflow of reserves (see Krueger, 1978, for a more detailed exposition of this scenario). In response to increasing shortages of imported intermediate goods, output growth also falls. Following devaluation, export revenues recover, but the authorities maintain constraints on import spending until their depleted stocks of reserves are restored. Subsequently, import and output growth respond positively and rise to their pre-devaluation levels, with the result that there is some deterioration in the reserves/imports ratio.

Both scenarios take as given the role of the real exchange rate in producing the sharp post-devaluation export response. As already noted, the short-term rebound in exports is surprising, and especially so if it represents an actual increase in the production of exportables in response to their increased relative price. Two explanations are worth exploring. First, the pattern of export growth revealed in the data may reflect responses to anticipations of devaluation. Firms may either store export goods or fail to declare and surrender export earnings prior to an expected devaluation. After the devaluation, firms either sell their accumulated inventory or resume reporting and surrendering their export receipts. Alternatively, contractionary policies associated with devaluations may depress the domestic demand for exportables and in that way expand the supply of goods for export. In either case, recorded exports will rise much more quickly than the production of exportables.

The information under examination here is not sufficient to discriminate completely between these interpretations of the devaluation process. In particular, the role of other stabilization policies—credit creation, fiscal management, and trade policy—must be brought to bear on these questions. Nevertheless, the data analyzed thus far do raise some issues for consideration.

First, the Keynesian/neoclassical scenario suggests that before the devaluation the marginal propensity to import should remain about constant or increase (owing to the appreciation of the real exchange rate); it should subsequently fall as a result of the devaluation. Table 10 indicates the move-

TABLE 10

SUMMARY RESULTS FOR IMPORTS/GDP RATIO

(57 *devaluations*)

	Year Relative to Devaluation Year T						
	$T-3$	$T-2$	$T-1$	T	$T+1$	$T+2$	$T+3$
Devaluing countries:							
Summary statistics:							
Mean	15.7	15.9	15.7	17.4	18.0	18.6	18.9
Median	14.1	13.7	12.1	14.4	15.4	16.2	16.5
Change from previous period:							
No. increasing		24	26	39	29	32	29
No. decreasing		33	31	18	28	25	28
Prob. if H_0 true		14.5	29.8	0.4	50.0	21.4	50.0
t-statistic		0.6	-0.8	3.2	1.6	2.0	0.7
Total sample:							
Summary statistics:							
Mean	16.1	16.3	16.7	17.1	17.2	17.6	18.1
Median	15.2	15.5	15.4	15.5	16.1	18.0	19.6
Change from previous period:							
No. increasing		32	33	31	30	33	33
No. decreasing		25	24	26	27	24	24
Prob. if H_0 true		21.4	14.5	29.8	39.6	14.5	14.5
t-statistic		1.3	2.1	2.1	1.3	2.1	2.7
Difference:							
Summary statistics:							
Mean	-0.4	-0.4	-1.0	0.3	0.7	1.0	0.8
Median	-1.1	-1.8	-3.3	-1.1	-0.6	-1.8	-3.0
Change from previous period:							
No. increasing		26	23	39	27	31	27
No. decreasing		31	34	18	30	26	30
Prob. if H_0 true		29.8	9.2	0.4	39.6	29.8	39.6
t-statistic		-0.0	-2.2	2.8	1.1	0.8	-0.6
Rank sum t-stat.		-0.6	-1.4	3.1	0.1	0.3	0.0

NOTE: Summary statistics and probabilities in percent.

ment of the imports/GDP ratio, or average propensity to import, over the course of the devaluation period. In absolute terms, the ratio remains virtually stable prior to devaluation and increases significantly thereafter. Relative to the comparison group, there is weak evidence that it falls in the year prior to devaluation before rising strongly in the next year. Appendix

34

Table A-10 offers weak evidence of a long-run increase in the average propensity to import relative to the entire sample. If this statistic is a reasonable proxy for the marginal propensity to import out of income, the evidence militates against the Keynesian/neoclassical scenario. It is, however, entirely consistent with the reserves-constraint approach. Here, initial import shortages force the imports/GDP ratio downward, but after the devaluation imports rise with the availability of foreign exchange, even though they are somewhat constrained by the efforts of the authorities to accumulate reserves.

A second way to distinguish between the two scenarios would be to see how imports, exports, output, and reserves performance "co-vary" during devaluation episodes. Although the key variables move together in aggregate over the devaluation period, there may be sufficient variation across devaluation episodes to test a number of implications of the Keynesian/neoclassical and reserves-constraint scenarios. To begin with, if the neoclassical model of trade determination is correct, the depreciation of the real exchange rate should be associated, *ceteris paribus*, with higher export growth and lower import growth. Second, if the Keynesian/neoclassical scenario is accurate, imports will be positively associated only with output growth and appreciations of the real exchange rate. If the reserves-constraint scenario is accurate, imports will also be associated with measures of foreign-exchange availability such as exports and reserves.

The accompanying table presents the results of cross-section regressions of changes in export and import growth on appropriate sets of explanatory variables for three periods of change: $T-2$ to $T-1$ (the initial deterioration), $T-1$ to T (the short-run effect of devaluation), and the average of $T-3$ and $T-2$ to the average of $T+1$, $T+2$, and $T+3$ (the long-run effect). The lagged reserves/imports ratio is used to avoid the simultaneous feedback of imports onto the contemporaneous ratio. In the export equation, GDP and imports are left out for the same reason. This exclusion is justified because both models take as given the exogeneity of exports with respect to GDP and imports. Finally, the real-exchange-rate level and the reserves/imports ratio are presumed to influence the growth rate of exports and imports. Hence, the growth of the real exchange rate and the change in the reserves/imports ratio are used to explain the change in the growth rates of exports and imports.

The regressions summarized in the table are extremely crude and can be regarded only as suggestive of particular relationships. Notwithstanding the low explanatory power of the two scenarios, the real exchange rate does appear to be a significant determinant of export performance in the deterioration and long-run periods. It is not significant in the short-run period. Perhaps expectation effects or changes in domestic demand are more im-

	Deterioration Period	Short Run	Long Run
Export growth:			
Regressors:			
Real exchange rate	0.53	0.09	0.11
	(2.97)	(0.70)	(2.05)
Reserves/imports ratio	0.01	0.02	0.01
	(0.58)	(−0.58)	(0.72)
Corrected R^2	0.14	−0.04	0.06
Import growth:			
Regressors:			
Export growth	0.22	0.07	0.29
	(1.72)	(0.47)	(2.14)
GDP growth	0.54	1.43	1.73
	(0.83)	(1.51)	(2.65)
Real exchange rate	0.09	0.06	−0.01
	(0.58)	(0.54)	(−0.22)
Reserves/imports ratio	0.09	0.08	0.07
	(4.92)	(3.69)	(4.42)
Corrected R^2	0.40	0.35	0.50

portant than the exchange-rate change itself in determining export behavior during the period immediately following devaluation.

Exchange-rate effects are unimportant in explaining changes in the growth rate of imports in all three periods. Conversely, the measures of foreign-exchange availability—export performance and especially the reserves/imports ratio—do appear to be associated significantly with import growth.

To reiterate, these regressions are extremely preliminary and no more than an initial attempt to make sense of some of the stylized trends identified in the data. The very low explanatory power of the equations indicates that much more work must be directed toward explaining the movements of key indicators during devaluation episodes. Nevertheless, the robust performance of the reserves/imports ratio in explaining imports, coupled with the behavior of the imports/GDP ratio described earlier, point strongly to some variant of the reserves-constraint scenario as a potential model of the devaluation process.

6 CONCLUSION

The findings of the research described here reveal certain patterns in the real external balance, the financial external balance, and internal macroeconomic performance when a country devalues its currency.

The trade balance typically deteriorates prior to devaluation, improves significantly in the year following devaluation, and then begins to decline again. While it shows net decline over the entire devaluation period, it declines by less than the trade balance of the total sample. The improvement in the trade balance is associated with an increase in export growth rather than a decrease in import growth. Both export and import growth fall in the year prior to devaluation, but export growth swings up in the first year after devaluation, while import growth increases in the second year after devaluation.

The current account largely reflects the behavior of the trade balance over the course of the devaluation period. The results confirm earlier findings by identifying both short- and long-term improvements in the balance of payments (as indicated by changes in reserves) after a devaluation. But they contradict other arguments in the literature by showing that these improvements are associated with improvements in the current account rather than in capital inflows. Capital inflows were found to grow more slowly for the devaluing countries than for the total sample.

While devaluations appear to be associated with temporary increases in inflation, their long-run impact on inflation rates may be very small. No support was found for the contention that the additional inflation caused by devaluations will entirely cancel out real depreciations. Devaluing countries tend to experience declines in output immediately *prior* to devaluations; no evidence was found that devaluations have a direct contractionary effect.

Preliminary as they are, these findings strongly suggest that devaluations may not be as ineffectual or as injurious as some critics have claimed. The external-balance performance of the devaluing countries compared very favorably with that of the nondevaluing countries and reflected neither drastic cutbacks in imports nor increased indebtedness to external creditors. While over the long term there was no evidence that devaluing countries cut back on imports more than their nondevaluing neighbors did, their reserves/imports ratios rose in relative terms. Moreover, no long-term deleterious effects on either inflation or output growth were identified.

Perhaps not surprisingly, the research may have uncovered as many significant differences between the devaluing countries and the comparison group in the years prior to the devaluations as in the years after. Most indices of performance—trade balance, reserves, output growth—were shown to deteriorate before countries devalued their currencies. Probably these countries faced different, harsher economic circumstances than those that maintained their exchange rate. Thus the currency devaluation itself should be regarded as merely one element in a larger devaluation episode or crisis. In consequence, both empirical and theoretical research should focus not on the impact of devaluations themselves but on the behavior of key indicators over the course of the devaluation period.

The analysis and regressions set out in Chapter 5 represent some extremely preliminary efforts in this direction. The poor explanatory power of the estimated equations suggests, first, that neither the Keynesian/neoclassical nor the reserves-constraint scenario of the devaluation process is entirely accurate. Perhaps more important, it calls attention to the need to bring information about other policy variables, and other elements of the policy environment, to bear on the issue. The findings refer to the effects of devaluation and stabilization programs applied in tandem and not to the effects of exchange-rate actions in isolation. Moreover, the findings cannot confirm any causal links between devaluations and economic performance; they merely highlight correlations between devaluations and performance indicators. Clearly, a great deal of additional research remains to be done on the effects of currency devaluations. In order to isolate these effects, the effects of associated trade and macroeconomic policies must be studied and accounted for. And in order to go beyond mere description and correlation, hypotheses must be developed and tested to explain the stylized trends discerned here.

REFERENCES

Bhagwat, Avinash, and Yusuke Onitsuka, "Export-Import Responses to Devaluation: Experience of the Non-Industrial Countries in the 1960's," *IMF Staff Papers*, 21 (July 1974), pp. 414-462.

Bird, Graham, "Should Developing Countries Use Currency Depreciation as a Tool of BOP Adjustment? A Review of Theory and Evidence, and a Guide for the Policy Maker," *Journal of Development Studies*, 19 (July 1983), pp. 461-484.

Connolly, Michael, and Dean Taylor, "Testing the Monetary Approach to Devaluation in Developing Countries," *Journal of Political Economy*, 84 (August 1976), pp. 849-860.

Cooper, Richard N., "An Assessment of Currency Devaluation in Developing Countries," in Gustav Ranis, ed., *Government and Economic Development*, New Haven, Yale University Press, 1971a.

——, *Currency Depreciation in Developing Countries*, Essays in International Finance No. 86, Princeton, N.J., Princeton University, International Finance Section, June 1971b.

Donovan, Donal J., "Real Responses Associated with Exchange Rate Action in Selected Upper Credit Tranche Stabilization Programs," *IMF Staff Papers*, 28 (December 1981), pp. 698-727.

Dornbusch, Rudiger, *Open Economy Macroeconomics*, New York, Basic Books, 1980.

Diaz-Alejandro, Carlos F., *Exchange Rate Devaluation in a Semi-Industrialized Economy: The Experience of Argentina 1955-61*, Cambridge, Mass., MIT Press, 1965.

Edwards, Sebastian, "Are Devaluations Contractionary?" NBER Working Paper Series No. 1676, August 1985.

——, "Exchange Controls, Devaluations and Real Exchange Rates: The Latin American Experience," Los Angeles, UCLA, 1987, unpublished.

Goldstein, Morris, "The Effects of Exchange Rate Changes on Wages and Prices in the United Kingdom: An Empirical Study," *IMF Staff Papers*, 21 (November 1974), pp. 694-739.

Gylfason, Thorvaldur, *Credit Policy and Economic Activity in Developing Countries with IMF Stabilization Programs*, Princeton Studies in International Finance No. 60, Princeton, N.J., Princeton University, International Finance Section, August 1987.

Gylfason, Thorvaldur, and Ole Risager, "Does Devaluation Improve the Current Account?" *European Economic Review*, 25 (June 1984), pp. 37-64.

Gylfason, Thorvaldur, and Michael Schmid, "Does Devaluation Cause Stagflation?" *Canadian Journal of Economics*, 16 (November 1983), pp. 641- 654.

Khan, M. S., "Import and Export Demand in Developing Countries," *IMF Staff Papers*, 21 (November 1974), pp. 678-693.

Krueger, Anne O., *Foreign Trade Regimes and Economic Development: Liberalization Attempts and Consequences*, Cambridge, Mass., Balinger, 1978.

Krugman, Paul, "A Model of Balance of Payments Crises," *Journal of Money, Credit and Banking*, 11 (August 1979), pp. 311-325.

Krugman, Paul, and Lance Taylor, "Contractionary Effects of Devaluation," *Journal of International Economics*, 8 (August 1978), pp. 445-456.

Lehmann, E. L., *Nonparametrics: Statistical Methods Based on Ranks*, San Francisco, Holden-Day, 1975.

Miles, Marc A., "The Effects of Devaluation on the Trade Balance and the Balance of Payments: Some New Results," *Journal of Political Economy*, 87 (June 1979), pp. 600-620.

Rabin, Alan A., and Leland B. Yeager, *Monetary Approaches to the Balance of Payments and Exchange Rates*, Essays in International Finance No. 148, Princeton, N.J., Princeton University, International Finance Section, November 1982.

Salant, Michael, "Devaluations Improve the Balance of Payments Even if Not the Trade Balance," in Peter Clark, Dennis Logue, and Richard J. Sweeney, eds., *The Effects of Exchange Rate Adjustments*, Washington, U.S. Department of the Treasury, 1976.

APPENDIX A

TESTS FOR LONGER-TERM CHANGES IN PERFORMANCE INDICATORS

TABLE A-1

TESTS FOR LONGER-TERM CHANGES IN SCALED TRADE BALANCE

(64 devaluations)

	Change in Period Average from Previous Period		
	T−3, T−2 to T+1, T+2, T+3	T−3, T−2 to T	T to T+1, T+2, T+3
Devaluing countries:			
No. increasing	25	33	30
No. decreasing	39	31	34
Prob. if H_0 true	5.2	45.0	35.4
t-statistic	−1.8	−0.9	−1.2
Total sample:			
No. increasing	11	21	19
No. decreasing	53	43	45
Prob. if H_0 true	0.0	0.4	0.1
t-statistic	−8.9	−4.7	−5.4
Difference:			
No. increasing	38	36	37
No. decreasing	26	28	27
Prob. if H_0 true	8.4	19.1	13.0
t-statistic	1.2	1.4	0.4
Rank sum t-stat.	2.0	1.6	1.3

NOTE: Probabilities in percent.

41

TABLE A-2

Tests for Longer-Term Changes in Import Growth
(64 devaluations)

	Change in Period Average from Previous Period		
	T−3, T−2 to T+1, T+2, T+3	T−3, T−2 to T	T to T+1, T+2, T+3
Devaluing countries:			
No. increasing	39	23	43
No. decreasing	25	41	21
Prob. if H_0 true	5.2	1.6	0.4
t-statistic	1.3	−2.1	3.4
Total sample:			
No. increasing	41	38	38
No. decreasing	23	26	26
Prob. if H_0 true	1.6	8.4	8.4
t-statistic	1.0	0.7	0.1
Difference:			
No. increasing	37	21	46
No. decreasing	27	43	18
Prob. if H_0 true	13.0	0.4	0.0
t-statistic	0.9	−3.4	4.3
Rank sum t-stat.	1.1	−3.4	4.4

NOTE: Probabilities in percent.

TABLE A-3

Tests for Longer-Term Changes in Export Growth
(64 devaluations)

	Change in Period Average from Previous Period		
	T−3, T−2 to T+1, T+2, T+3	T−3, T−2 to T	T to T+1, T+2, T+3
Devaluing countries:			
No. increasing	42	41	34
No. decreasing	22	23	30
Prob. if H_0 true	0.8	1.6	35.4
t-statistic	2.6	0.9	1.4
Total sample:			
No. increasing	33	41	36
No. decreasing	31	23	28
Prob. if H_0 true	45.0	1.6	19.1
t-statistic	−0.4	0.6	−1.0
Difference:			
No. increasing	41	39	37
No. decreasing	23	25	27
Prob. if H_0 true	1.6	5.2	13.0
t-statistic	3.3	0.8	2.2
Rank sum t-stat.	3.0	1.2	1.7

NOTE: Probabilities in percent.

42

TABLE A-4

Tests for Longer-Term Changes in Export-Price Growth

(51 devaluations)

	Change in Period Average from Previous Period		
	T−3, T−2 to T+1, T+2, T+3	T−3, T−2 to T	T to T+1, T+2, T+3
Devaluing countries:			
No. increasing	28	28	28
No. decreasing	23	23	23
Prob. if H_0 true	28.8	28.8	28.8
t-statistic	0.1	0.7	−0.7
Total sample:			
No. increasing	25	33	30
No. decreasing	26	18	21
Prob. if H_0 true	50.0	2.4	13.1
t-statistic	−0.2	−0.5	0.4
Difference:			
No. increasing	24	32	25
No. decreasing	27	19	26
Prob. if H_0 true	39.0	4.6	50.0
t-statistic	0.4	1.0	−0.9
Rank sum t-stat.	−0.1	1.1	−1.2

NOTE: Probabilities in percent.

TABLE A-5

Tests for Longer-Term Changes in Scaled Capital Inflows

(62 devaluations)

	Change in Period Average from Previous Period		
	T−3, T−2 to T+1, T+2, T+3	T−3, T−2 to T	T to T+1, T+2, T+3
Devaluing countries:			
No. increasing	45	36	40
No. decreasing	17	26	22
Prob. if H_0 true	0.0	12.6	1.5
t-statistic	4.0	1.5	2.3
Total sample:			
No. increasing	55	51	52
No. decreasing	7	11	10
Prob. if H_0 true	0.0	0.0	0.0
t-statistic	12.3	8.2	7.8
Difference:			
No. increasing	20	26	29
No. decreasing	42	36	33
Prob. if H_0 true	0.4	12.6	35.2
t-statistic	−1.0	−1.3	0.1
Rank sum t-stat.	−2.0	−1.5	−0.1

NOTE: Probabilities in percent.

TABLE A-6

Tests for Longer-Term Changes in Scaled Reserves Outflows
(65 devaluations)

	Change in Period Average from Previous Period		
	T−3, T−2 to T+1, T+2, T+3	T−3, T−2 to T	T to T+1, T+2, T+3
Devaluing countries:			
No. increasing	19	28	23
No. decreasing	46	37	42
Prob. if H_0 true	0.1	16.1	1.2
t-statistic	−2.8	−1.0	−1.1
Total sample:			
No. increasing	29	18	34
No. decreasing	36	47	31
Prob. if H_0 true	22.9	0.0	40.2
t-statistic	−0.8	−2.5	1.3
Difference:			
No. increasing	22	34	21
No. decreasing	43	31	44
Prob. if H_0 true	0.6	40.2	0.3
t-statistic	−2.8	−0.4	−1.7
Rank sum t-stat.	−2.6	0.4	−2.2

NOTE: Probabilities in percent.

TABLE A-7

Tests for Longer-Term Changes in CPI Growth
(74 devaluations)

	Change in Period Average from Previous Period		
	T−3, T−2 to T+1, T+2, T+3	T−3, T−2 to T	T to T+1, T+2, T+3
Devaluing countries:			
No. increasing	47	53	36
No. decreasing	27	21	38
Prob. if H_0 true	1.3	0.0	45.4
t-statistic	1.4	2.0	−0.2
Total sample:			
No. increasing	50	45	48
No. decreasing	24	29	26
Prob. if H_0 true	0.2	4.0	0.7
t-statistic	4.7	1.9	3.2
Difference:			
No. increasing	45	55	29
No. decreasing	29	19	45
Prob. if H_0 true	4.0	0.0	4.0
t-statistic	1.1	1.9	−0.6
Rank sum t-stat.	0.9	4.9	−3.6

NOTE: Probabilities in percent.

44

TABLE A-8

Tests for Longer-Term Changes in Real Exchange Rates

(72 *devaluations*)

	Change in Period Average from Previous Period		
	T − 3, T − 2 to T + 1, T + 2, T + 3	T − 3, T − 2 to T	T to T + 1, T + 2, T + 3
Devaluing countries:			
No. increasing	32	42	16
No. decreasing	40	30	56
Prob. if H_0 true	20.5	9.7	0.0
t-statistic	− 0.0	2.7	− 3.5
Total sample:			
No. increasing	8	17	12
No. decreasing	64	55	60
Prob. if H_0 true	0.0	0.0	0.0
t-statistic	− 10.7	− 7.9	− 9.1
Difference:			
No. increasing	54	56	28
No. decreasing	18	16	44
Prob. if H_0 true	0.0	0.0	3.8
t-statistic	5.7	6.9	0.1
Rank sum t-stat.	6.4	7.4	− 1.1

NOTE: Probabilities in percent.

TABLE A-9

Tests for Longer-Term Changes in Real GDP Growth

(60 *devaluations*)

	Change in Period Average from Previous Period		
	T − 3, T − 2 to T + 1, T + 2, T + 3	T − 3, T − 2 to T	T to T + 1, T + 2, T + 3
Devaluing countries:			
No. increasing	28	25	33
No. decreasing	32	35	27
Prob. if H_0 true	34.9	12.3	25.9
t-statistic	− 1.2	− 2.4	1.5
Total sample:			
No. increasing	21	27	25
No. decreasing	39	33	35
Prob. if H_0 true	1.4	25.9	12.3
t-statistic	− 2.8	− 1.6	− 1.5
Difference:			
No. increasing	32	24	41
No. decreasing	28	36	19
Prob. if H_0 true	34.9	7.7	0.3
t-statistic	− 0.5	− 2.1	1.9
Rank sum t-stat.	− 0.4	− 1.6	1.8

NOTE: Probabilities in percent.

TABLE A-10

TESTS FOR LONGER-TERM CHANGES IN IMPORTS/GDP RATIO

(57 devaluations)

	Change in Period Average from Previous Period		
	T−3, T−2 to T+1, T+2, T+3	T−3, T−2 to T	T to T+1, T+2, T+3
Devaluing countries:			
No. increasing	43	35	34
No. decreasing	14	22	23
Prob. if H_0 true	0.0	5.6	9.2
t-statistic	3.9	2.8	2.3
Total sample:			
No. increasing	47	31	31
No. decreasing	10	26	26
Prob. if H_0 true	0.0	29.8	29.8
t-statistic	5.7	3.1	2.8
Difference:			
No. increasing	33	31	28
No. decreasing	24	26	29
Prob. if H_0 true	14.5	29.8	50.0
t-statistic	1.8	1.3	1.2
Rank sum *t*-stat.	1.9	1.8	0.6

NOTE: Probabilities in percent.

APPENDIX B

DATA DESCRIPTION AND SOURCES

TABLE B-1

THE DEVALUATION SAMPLE

(in percent)

Devaluing Country	Devaluation Date	Depreciation Rate	Previous Year's Inflation
Afghanistan	3/63	125	...
Argentina	4/62	63	...
Argentina	3/75	160	120
Argentina	7/82	175	...
Bangladesh	5/75	73	39
Bolivia	10/58	31	13
Bolivia	10/72	68	6
Bolivia	11/79	23	19
Bolivia	2/82	76	...
Bolivia	11/82	354	...
Bolivia	12/83	155	...
Botswana	9/75	22	...
Brazil	9/64	34	78
Burma	1/75	30	26
Burundi	1/65	75	...
Burundi	5/76	14	12
Burundi	11/83	30	...
Chile	11/54	...	...
Chile	10/62	45	...
Chile	12/71	30	...
Chile	8/72	58	...
Chile	10/73	1,340	...
Chile	6/82	19	...
Colombia	11/62	34	3
Colombia	9/65	50	7
Costa Rica	9/61	15	2
Costa Rica	4/74	29	21
Costa Rica	1/81	88	...
Egypt	5/62	24	−1
Egypt	1/79	79	11
Ghana	6/67	43	0

Continued on next page

Devaluing Country	Devaluation Date	Depreciation Rate	Previous Year's Inflation
Ghana	12/71	78	9
Ghana	8/78	104	81
Ghana	10/83	991	...
Greece	4/53	50	6
Guyana	6/81	18	...
India	6/66	58	10
Indonesia	4/70	16	16
Indonesia	11/78	51	8
Indonesia	4/83	39	...
Israel	1/54–9/54	...	32
Israel	2/62	67	6
Israel	8/71	20	11
Israel	11/74	43	37
Israel	11/77	50	34
Jamaica	5/78	50	22
Jamaica	11/83	84	...
Kenya	9/81	18	...
Kenya	12/82	14	...
Korea	7/55–9/55	...	60
Korea	2/60	30	4
Korea	2/61	100	10
Korea	5/64	97	24
Korea	12/74	21	24
Korea	1/80	21	19
Lesotho	9/75	22	...
Mexico	4/54	31	...
Mexico	9/76	59	16
Mexico	2/82	73	...
Morocco	10/59	17	1
Nepal	12/67	33	...
Nepal	10/75	18	9
Nicaragua	4/79	43	20
Pakistan	7/55	30	−1
Pakistan	5/72	130	7
Paraguay	8/54	...	36
Paraguay	3/56	...	23
Peru	1/58	19	7
Peru	10/67	43	10
Peru	9/75	16	22
Peru	6/76	44	29
Phillipines	1/62	82	2
Phillipines	2/70	55	4

48

TABLE B-1 *(Continued)*

Devaluing Country	Devaluation Date	Depreciation Rate	Previous Year's Inflation
Phillipines	10/83	27	...
Rwanda	4/66	100	...
Sierra Leone	7/83	96	...
Somalia	7/82	142	...
South Africa	9/75	22	13
Spain	7/59	14	10
Spain	8/77	22	22
Sri Lanka	11/77	81	1
Sudan	6/78	15	18
Sudan	9/79	25	29
Sudan	11/81	80	...
Sudan	11/82	44	...
Swaziland	9/75	22	14
Tanzania	10/75	16	25
Tanzania	6/83	25	...
Tunisia	9/64	24	4
Turkey	8/58	167	19
Turkey	8/70	65	7
Turkey	3/78	30	32
Turkey	6/79	40	53
Turkey	1/80	100	65
Uruguay	5/63	45	...
Uruguay	11/67	102	92
Uruguay	4/68	25	125
Uruguay	12/71	48	25
Uruguay	11/82	45	...
Venezuela	1/64	38	1
Yugoslavia	7/65	67	25
Yugoslavia	1/71	20	10
Yugoslavia	6/80	35	26
Zambia	7/76	24	15
Mean		76	22
Standard deviation		164	26
Median		43	15

NOTE: Depreciation rates calculated from IFS line code "ae," end-of-period quarterly nominal exchange rates. In the case of devaluations for which these data were not available, other series or previously published work was used to identify the devaluation.

Variables are listed in the order of presentation within text. IFS refers to the IMF's *International Financial Statistics*. Unless otherwise noted, all data were found in the IMF's monthly IFSDATA tape.

1. Trade balance: Merchandise exports minus merchandise imports.
2. Imports: Current-dollar merchandise imports f.o.b. IFS line code 77abd.
3. Import prices: Import unit values. IFS line code 75d.
4. Exports: Current-dollar merchandise exports f.o.b. IFS line code 77aad.
5. Current-account balance: Net exports of goods and services, plus net transfers. IFS line code 77a.d.
6. Capital inflows: The current-account deficit minus reserves movements: $-(77a.d. + 79c.d.)$.
7. Reserves outflows: Total changes in reserves. IFS line code 79c.d.
8. Reserves levels: Total reserves minus gold. IFS line code 11.d.
9. CPI: Consumer price index. IFS line code 64.
10. Exchange rate: Annual average, par rate/market rate, local currency per dollar. IFS line code rf.
11. Real-exchange-rate index: For year T:
    [Exchange rate (T)/CPI(T)]/[exchange rate(1975)/CPI(1975)].
12. Nominal GDP: IFS line code 99b.
13. Real GDP: IFS line code 99b.p.

PUBLICATIONS OF THE
INTERNATIONAL FINANCE SECTION

Notice to Contributors

The International Finance Section publishes at irregular intervals papers in four series: ESSAYS IN INTERNATIONAL FINANCE, PRINCETON STUDIES IN INTERNATIONAL FINANCE, SPECIAL PAPERS IN INTERNATIONAL ECONOMICS, and REPRINTS IN INTERNATIONAL FINANCE. ESSAYS and STUDIES are confined to subjects in international finance. SPECIAL PAPERS are surveys of the literature suitable for courses in colleges and universities.

An ESSAY should be a lucid exposition of a theme, accessible not only to the professional economist but to other interested readers. It should therefore avoid technical terms, should eschew mathematics and statistical tables (except when essential for an understanding of the text), and should rarely have footnotes.

A STUDY or SPECIAL PAPER may be more technical. It may include statistics and algebra and may have many footnotes. STUDIES and SPECIAL PAPERS may also be longer than ESSAYS; indeed, these two series are meant to accommodate manuscripts too long for journal articles and too short for books.

To facilitate prompt evaluation, please submit three copies of your manuscript. Retain one for your files. The manuscript should be typed on one side of 8½ by 11 strong white paper. All material should be double-spaced—text, excerpts, footnotes, tables, references, and figure legends. For more complete guidance, prospective contributors should send for the Section's style guide before preparing their manuscripts.

How to Obtain Publications

A mailing list is maintained for free distribution of all new publications to college, university, and public libraries and nongovernmental, nonprofit research institutions.

Individuals and organizations not qualifying for free distribution can receive all publications—ESSAYS, STUDIES, SPECIAL PAPERS, and REPRINTS—by paying a fee of $30 (inside and outside U.S.) to cover the period January 1 through December 31, 1988.

ESSAYS and REPRINTS can also be ordered from the Section at $4.50 per copy, and STUDIES and SPECIAL PAPERS at $6.50. Payment MUST be included with the order and MUST be made in U.S. dollars. PLEASE INCLUDE $1.25 FOR POSTAGE AND HANDLING. (These charges are waived on orders from persons or organizations in countries whose foreign-exchange regulations prohibit such remittances.) For airmail delivery outside U.S., Canada, and Mexico, there is an additional charge of $1.50.

All manuscripts, correspondence, and orders should be addressed to:
International Finance Section
Department of Economics, Dickinson Hall
Princeton University
Princeton, New Jersey 08544

Subscribers should notify the Section promptly of a change of address, giving the old address as well as the new one.

List of Recent Publications

To obtain a complete list of publications, write the International Finance Section.

ESSAYS IN INTERNATIONAL FINANCE

147. Edmar Lisboa Bacha and Carlos F. Díaz Alejandro, *International Financial Intermediation: A Long and Tropical View*. (May 1982)
148. Alan A. Rabin and Leland B. Yeager, *Monetary Approaches to the Balance of Payments and Exchange Rates*. (Nov. 1982)
149. C. Fred Bergsten, Rudiger Dornbusch, Jacob A. Frenkel, Steven W. Kohlhagen, Luigi Spaventa, and Thomas D. Willett, *From Rambouillet to Versailles: A Symposium*. (Dec. 1982)
150. Robert E. Baldwin, *The Inefficacy of Trade Policy*. (Dec. 1982)
151. Jack Guttentag and Richard Herring, *The Lender-of-Last Resort Function in an International Context*. (May 1983)
152. G. K. Helleiner, *The IMF and Africa in the 1980s*. (July 1983)
153. Rachel McCulloch, *Unexpected Real Consequences of Floating Exchange Rates*. (Aug. 1983)
154. Robert M. Dunn, Jr., *The Many Disappointments of Floating Exchange Rates*. (Dec. 1983)
155. Stephen Marris, *Managing the World Economy: Will We Ever Learn?* (Oct. 1984)
156. Sebastian Edwards, *The Order of Liberalization of the External Sector in Developing Countries*. (Dec. 1984)
157. Wilfred J. Ethier and Richard C. Marston, eds., with Kindleberger, Guttentag and Herring, Wallich, Henderson, and Hinshaw, *International Financial Markets and Capital Movements: A Symposium in Honor of Arthur I. Bloomfield*. (Sept. 1985)
158. Charles E. Dumas, *The Effects of Government Deficits: A Comparative Analysis of Crowding Out*. (Oct. 1985)
159. Jeffrey A. Frankel, *Six Possible Meanings of "Overvaluation": The 1981-85 Dollar*. (Dec. 1985)
160. Stanley W. Black, *Learning from Adversity: Policy Responses to Two Oil Shocks*. (Dec. 1985)
161. Alexis Rieffel, *The Role of the Paris Club in Managing Debt Problems*. (Dec. 1985)
162. Stephen E. Haynes, Michael M. Hutchison, and Raymond F. Mikesell, *Japanese Financial Policies and the U.S. Trade Deficit*. (April 1986)
163. Arminio Fraga, *German Reparations and Brazilian Debt: A Comparative Study*. (July 1986)
164. Jack M. Guttentag and Richard J. Herring, *Disaster Myopia in International Banking*. (Sept. 1986)
165. Rudiger Dornbusch, *Inflation, Exchange Rates, and Stabilization*. (Oct. 1986)
166. John Spraos, *IMF Conditionality: Ineffectual, Inefficient, Mistargeted*. (Dec. 1986)
167. Rainer Stefano Masera, *An Increasing Role for the ECU: A Character in Search of a Script*. (June 1987)
168. Paul Mosley, *Conditionality as Bargaining Process: Structural-Adjustment Lending, 1980-86*. (Oct. 1987)
169. Paul A. Volcker, Ralph C. Bryant, Leonhard Gleske, Gottfried Haberler, Al-

exandre Lamfalussy, Shijuro Ogata, Jesús Silva-Herzog, Ross M. Starr, James Tobin, and Robert Triffin, *International Monetary Cooperation: Essays in Honor of Henry C. Wallich*. (Dec. 1987)

170. Shafiqul Islam, *The Dollar and the Policy-Performance-Confidence Mix*. (July 1988)

PRINCETON STUDIES IN INTERNATIONAL FINANCE

49. Peter Bernholz, *Flexible Exchange Rates in Historical Perspective*. (July 1982)
50. Victor Argy, *Exchange-Rate Management in Theory and Practice*. (Oct. 1982)
51. Paul Wonnacott, *U.S. Intervention in the Exchange Market for DM, 1977-80*. (Dec. 1982)
52. Irving B. Kravis and Robert E. Lipsey, *Toward an Explanation of National Price Levels*. (Nov. 1983)
53. Avraham Ben-Bassat, *Reserve-Currency Diversification and the Substitution Account*. (March 1984)
*54. Jeffrey Sachs, *Theoretical Issues in International Borrowing*. (July 1984)
55. Marsha R. Shelburn, *Rules for Regulating Intervention under a Managed Float*. (Dec. 1984)
56. Paul De Grauwe, Marc Janssens, and Hilde Leliaert, *Real-Exchange-Rate Variability from 1920 to 1926 and 1973 to 1982*. (Sept. 1985)
57. Stephen S. Golub, *The Current-Account Balance and the Dollar: 1977-78 and 1983-84*. (Oct. 1986)
58. John T. Cuddington, *Capital Flight: Estimates, Issues, and Explanations*. (Dec. 1986)
59. Vincent P. Crawford, *International Lending, Long-Term Credit Relationships, and Dynamic Contract Theory*. (March 1987)
60. Thorvaldur Gylfason, *Credit Policy and Economic Activity in Developing Countries with IMF Stabilization Programs*. (August 1987)
61. Stephen A. Schuker, *American "Reparations" to Germany, 1919-33: Implications for the Third-World Debt Crisis*. (July 1988)
62. Steven B. Kamin, *Devaluation, External Balance, and Macroeconomic Performance: A Look at the Numbers*. (August 1988)

SPECIAL PAPERS IN INTERNATIONAL ECONOMICS

13. Louka T. Katseli-Papaefstratiou, *The Reemergence of the Purchasing Power Parity Doctrine in the 1970s*. (Dec. 1979)
*14. Morris Goldstein, *Have Flexible Exchange Rates Handicapped Macroeconomic Policy?* (June 1980)
15. Gene M. Grossman and J. David Richardson, *Strategic Trade Policy: A Survey of Issues and Early Analysis*. (April 1985)

* Out of print. Available on demand in xerographic paperback or library-bound copies from University Microfilms International, Box 1467, Ann Arbor, Michigan 48106, United States, and 30-32 Mortimer St., London, WIN 7RA, England. Paperback reprints are usually $20. Microfilm of all Essays by year is also available from University Microfilms. Photocopied sheets of out-of-print titles are available on demand from the Section at $6 per Essay and $8 per Study or Special Paper.

22. Jorge Braga de Macedo, *Exchange Rate Behavior with Currency Inconvertibility*. [Reprinted from *Journal of International Economics*, 12 (Feb. 1982).] (Sept. 1982)

23. Peter B. Kenen, *Use of the SDR to Supplement or Substitute for Other Means of Finance*. [Reprinted from George M. von Furstenberg, ed., *International Money and Credit: The Policy Roles*, Washington, IMF, 1983, Chap. 7.] (Dec. 1983)

24. Peter B. Kenen, *Forward Rates, Interest Rates, and Expectations under Alternative Exchange Rate Regimes*. [Reprinted from *Economic Record*, 61 (Sept. 1985).] (June 1986)

25. Jorge Braga de Macedo, *Trade and Financial Interdependence under Flexible Exchange Rates: The Pacific Area*. [Reprinted from Augustine H.H. Tan and Basant Kapur, eds., *Pacific Growth and Financial Interdependence*, Sydney, Australia, Allen and Unwin, 1986, Chap. 13.] (June 1986)

ISBN 0-88165-234-2